Reed

The Concord and the Merrimack

Henry David Thoreau

The Concord and the Merrimack

Excerpts from

A WEEK ON THE CONCORD AND MERRIMACK RIVERS

Arranged with Notes by DUDLEY C. LUNT

Illustrated by Henry Bugbee Kane

BRAMHALL HOUSE · NEW YORK

LIBRARY OF CONGRESS CATALOG CARD NO. 54-11126

This edition published by Bramhall House,
a division of Clarkson N. Potter, Inc.
a b c d e f g h

PRINTED IN THE UNITED STATES OF AMERICA

I asked him the meaning of the word *Musketicook,* the Indian name of Concord River. He pronounced it *Muskéeticook,* emphasizing the second syllable with a peculiar guttural sound, and said that it meant "Dead-water," which it is.

THOREAU in conversation with the Penobscot Indian, Joe Polis, in *The Maine Woods,* July 24, 1857.

The Indians tells us of a beautiful River lying far to the south, which they call Merrimack.

SIEUR DE MONTS
Relations of the Jesuits, 1604.

Contents

Introductory Note

THE VALLEY of the Concord is no longer the remote and quiet countryside that was known to Thoreau. It has been utterly transformed into a rolling suburban development, laced and relaced by the broad black ribbands of high-speed highways. The same thing is true of the valley of the Merrimack. Only the form differs. Here the mill towns have taken over with stretches of open country between them. Today in your car you may cover in a day the entire itinerary followed by the brothers Thoreau in their small boat when they devoted a week to it on the Concord and the Merrimack Rivers. It is an interesting experience.

A placid, winding deadwater — that is the Concord River. You start with a look across the old North Bridge to where the embattled farmers stood. In swift succession comes a series of vistas up and down the Great Meadows, with a crossing of Carlisle Bridge thrown in, and then on to locate their first campground. Next the deadwater ends abruptly at a dam; and here you are in for a fascinating bit of exploration, particularly if you have a topographic map along. For then you can trace out the course and in many places find the bed of the century-and-a-half-old Middlesex Canal, and follow it to where it came out on the Merrimack in Middlesex Village.

The Merrimack is a rugged stream, swift-flowing, powerful. Gliding along the highways that line its banks you catch quick glimpses of blue water coursing between high banks. The river is never far distant, and it is but a step down to locate the site of a campground or to inspect the ruined remains of some ancient lock. Many a scene described by Thoreau is easily identifiable, such as the old Dunstable graveyard where lie so many victims of the French and Indian Wars. To this the mills of Nashua and Manchester stand in sharp contrast; above the latter city you come in the late afternoon to the end of your excursion, at Hookset Falls. Here there rises from the west bank, almost sheer to a height of three hundred feet, a towering granite pile — the Hookset Pinnacle.

"I have sat upon its summit, a precipitous rock only a few rods long, in fairer weather, when the sun was setting and filling the river valley with a flood of light. You can see up and down the Merrimack several miles each way. The broad and straight river, full of light and life, with its sparkling and foaming falls, the islet which divides the stream, the village of Hookset on the shore almost directly under your feet, so near that you can converse with its inhabitants or throw a stone into its yards, the woodland lake at its western base, and the mountains in the north and northeast, make a sense of rare beauty and completeness, which the traveler should take pains to behold."

So it is today and so wrote Thoreau in the year 1839, that year of destiny preceding the opening of a decade pregnant beyond belief with meaning for the future of American life. In that year the iron tentacles of the railroads were beginning to stretch their rights of way through New England and by that year the peak had been reached and there had commenced the decline of a development in the Concord and Merrimack valleys which had been assiduously cultivated for half a century. This was the opening by the Proprietors of the Middlesex Canal of access to the sea from the fertile and productive back country. In that early era and area, personal transportation by stagecoach and hauling by team aside, the bulk of man's commerce had come to be water-borne — down the streams, through the canals and on the high seas. And it was during this period of water-borne commerce that the brothers Thoreau embarked upon their excursion.

The installations on the Merrimack, which descends to the sea in a succession of deadwaters, falls and rapids, tell the tale. A few miles below Concord in New Hampshire, the Bow Canal used to lead around Garvin's Falls, access to it being by locks, and this was repeated nine miles below at Hookset Falls. Next Amoskeag Falls, at the present site of Manchester, descending in three pitches — fifty-four feet in half a mile — were bypassed by a mile long canal. Below there, several smaller falls and rapids had been locked. At length, just above Pawtucket Falls at

Lowell, there was the entrance, again by means of locks, into the Middlesex Canal. This system, fed by the waters of the Concord River, led through the eastern part of the county of that name, traversing valleys and crossing rivers — the Shawsheen aqueduct, for example, being thirty feet in the air supported upon stone pillars — to mingle ultimately with the waters of Boston Harbor. Since the year 1814 lumber, lime, granite, bricks and all the produce of the Merrimack watershed, and of the hinterland in "up-country" New Hampshire and Vermont, had moved by raft and canal boat to the markets and port of Boston. And in reverse there flowed steadily back into the interior all the traffic in what was then known as West India goods.

This was the milieu in which Thoreau's first reported excursion took place. In this setting, what an English reviewer has termed his "quality of lazy energy, his acute observation and his sensitive fidelity of reporting" have the fullest scope. Who will forget the mathematical lockman, or the canal boat that "was seen stealing mysteriously through the meadows and past the village"? Then there is his indelible vignette of the travelers waiting to cross on a ferry early on a Monday morning. There are his visits to the homes of the lockmen. His descriptions of ancient Indian campgrounds link the river traffic of his time and of ours to those olden times when New England's rivers were the homes of New England's Indians. Or regard the canal-boat man — "a brawny New Hampshire man, leaning on his pole, bareheaded and in shirt and trousers only, a rude Apollo of a man, coming down from that vast 'up-landish country' to the main; of nameless age, with flaxen hair, and vigorous, weather-bleached countenance, in whose wrinkles the sun still lodged, as little touched by the heats and frosts and withering cares of life, as a maple of the mountain."

All this was in 1839. Then, at some point in the year before publication a decade later, Thoreau revisited many of the scenes of the earlier excursion. Tremendous changes had taken place. The picturesque water-borne traffic, the fleets of canal boats creeping up and flowing downstream close to the banks to be locked past the falls, this was all but gone — just a few sporadic trips between neighboring towns. The canals and locks could no longer be supported by the tolls and were falling into disrepair and disuse. In 1839 in camp below Nashua, Thoreau had recorded that "we were kept awake by the boisterous sport of some Irish laborers on the railroad wafted to us over the water." In 1849 this railroad had been extended and now ran from Boston to Concord in New Hampshire and beyond. And Thoreau records that the river's " . . . real vessels are railroad cars, and its true and main stream, flowing by an iron channel further south, may be traced by a long line of vapor amid the hills, which no morning wind ever disperses, to where it empties into the sea at Boston. This side is the louder murmur now. Instead of the scream of the fish-hawk scaring the fishes, is heard the whistle of the steam engine, arousing a country to its progress."

There it is. A slice of American life that is completely lost to us, here caught in perfect focus in the prose of a master.

"At length," recorded Henry, "on Saturday, the last day of August, 1839, we two, brothers, and natives of Concord, weighed anchor in this river port. . . . With a vigorous shove we launched our boat."

DUDLEY C. LUNT

Wilmington, Delaware

The Concord and the Merrimack

1. *Concord River*

The Musketaquid, or Grass-ground River, though probably as old as the Nile or Euphrates, did not begin to have a place in civilized history until the fame of its grassy meadows and its fish attracted settlers out of England in 1635, when it received the other but kindred name of Concord from the first plantation on its banks, which appears to have been commenced in a spirit of peace and harmony. It will be Grass-ground River as long as grass grows and water runs here; it will be Concord River only while men lead peaceable lives on its banks. To an extinct race it was grass-ground, where they hunted and fished; and it is still perennial grass-ground to Concord farmers, who own the Great Meadows, and get the hay from year to year.

"One branch of it," according to the historian of Concord, for I love to quote so good authority, "rises in the south part of Hopkinton, and another from a pond and a large cedar-swamp in Westborough," and flowing between Hopkinton and Southborough, through Framingham, and between Sudbury and Wayland, where it is sometimes called Sudbury River, it enters Concord at the south part of the town, and after receiving the North or Assabet River, which has its source a little farther to the north and west, goes out at the northeast angle, and flowing between Bedford and Carlisle, and through Billerica, empties into the Merrimack at Lowell.

In Concord, it is in summer from four to fifteen feet deep, and from one hundred to three hundred feet wide, but in the spring freshets, when it overflows its banks, it is in some places nearly a mile wide. Between Sudbury and Wayland the meadows acquire their greatest breadth, and when covered with water, they form a handsome chain of shallow vernal lakes, resorted to by numerous gulls and ducks. Just above Sherman's Bridge, between these towns, is the largest expanse; and when the wind blows freshly in a raw March day, heaving up the surface into dark and sober billows or regular swells, skirted as it is in the distance with alder-swamps and smoke-like maples, it looks like a smaller Lake Huron, and is very pleasant and exciting for a landsman to row or sail over.

The farm-houses along the Sudbury shore, which rises gently to a considerable height, command fine water prospects at this season. The shore is more flat on the Wayland side, and this town is the greatest loser by the flood. Its farmers tell me that thousands of acres are flooded now, since the dams have been erected, where they remember to have seen the white honeysuckle or clover growing once, and they could go dry with shoes only in summer. Now there is nothing but blue-joint and sedge and cut-grass there, standing in water all the year round. For a long time, they made the most of the driest season to get their hay, working sometimes till nine o'clock at night, sedulously paring with their scythes in the twilight round the hummocks left by the ice; but now it is not worth the getting when they can come at it, and they look sadly round to their wood-lots and upland as a last resource.

It is worth the while to make a voyage up this stream, if you go no farther than Sudbury, only to see how much country there is in the rear of us: great hills, and a hundred brooks, and farm-houses, and barns, and haystacks, you never saw before, and men everywhere; Sudbury, that is *Southborough* men, and Wayland, and Nine-Acre-Corner men, and Bound Rock, where four towns bound on a rock in the river, Lincoln, Wayland, Sudbury, Concord.

Many waves are there agitated by the wind, keeping nature fresh, the spray blowing in your face, reeds and rushes waving; ducks by the hundred, all uneasy in the surf, in the raw wind, just ready to rise, and now going off with a clatter and a whistling like riggers straight for Labrador, flying against the stiff gale with reefed wings, or else circling round first, with all their paddles briskly moving, just over the surf, to reconnoitre you before they leave these parts; gulls wheeling overhead, muskrats swimming for dear life, wet and cold, with no fire to warm them by that you know of, their labored homes rising here and there like haystacks; and countless mice and moles and winged titmice along the sunny, windy shore; cranberries tossed on the waves and heaving up on the beach, their little red skiffs beating about among the alders; — such healthy natural tumult as proves the last day is not yet at hand. And there stand all around the alders, and birches, and oaks, and maples full of glee and sap, holding in their buds until the waters subside.

You shall perhaps run aground on Cranberry Island, only some spires of last year's pipe-grass above water to show where the danger is, and get as good a freezing there as anywhere on the Northwest Coast. I never voyaged so far in all my life. You shall see men you never heard of before, whose names you don't know, going away down through the meadows with long ducking-guns, with water-tight boots wading through the fowl-meadow grass, on bleak, wintry, distant shores, with guns at half-

cock; and they shall see teal, — blue-winged, green-winged, — shelldrakes, whistlers, black ducks, ospreys, and many other wild and noble sights before night, such as they who sit in parlors never dream of.

You shall see rude and sturdy, experienced and wise men, keeping their castles, or teaming up their summer's wood, or chopping alone in the woods; men fuller of talk and rare adventure in the sun and wind and rain, than a chestnut is of meat, who were out not only in '75 and 1812, but have been out every day of their lives; greater men than Homer, or Chaucer, or Shakespeare, only they never got time to say so; they never took to the way of writing. Look at their fields, and imagine what they might write, if ever they should put pen to paper. Or what have they not written on the face of the earth already, clearing, and burning, and scratching, and harrowing, and ploughing, and subsoiling, in and in, and out and out, and over and over, again and again, erasing what they had already written for want of parchment.

As yesterday and the historical ages are past, as the work of to-day is present, so some flitting perspectives and demi-experiences of the life that is in nature are in time veritably future, or rather outside to time, perennial, young, divine, in the wind and rain which never die.

Concord River is remarkable for the gentleness of its current, which is scarcely perceptible, and some have referred to its influence the proverbial moderation of the inhabitants of Concord, as exhibited in the Revolution, and on later occasions. It has been proposed that the town should adopt for its coat of arms a field verdant, with the Concord circling nine times round. I have read that a descent of an eighth of an inch in a mile is sufficient to produce a flow. Our river has, probably, very near the smallest allowance. The story is current, at any rate, though I believe that strict history will not bear it out, that the only bridge ever carried away on the main branch, within the limits of the town, was driven upstream by the wind. But wherever it makes a sudden bend it is shallower and swifter, and asserts its title to be called a river.

Compared with the other tributaries of the Merrimack, it appears to have been properly named Musketaquid, or Meadow River, by the Indians.[1] For the most part, it

---

[1] In the course of Thoreau's later excursions in the Maine woods he sought to satisfy his curiosity as to the meaning of "Musketaquid." In September, 1853, while camping with a group of Indians where the Northeast Carry from Moosehead Lake comes out on the West Branch of the Penobscot, "I asked our hosts what *Musketaquid*, the Indian name of Concord, Massachusetts, meant; but they changed it to *Musketicook*, and repeated that, and Tahmunt said that it meant Dead stream, which is probably true. *Cook* appears to mean stream, and perhaps *quid* signifies the place or ground." On his last river trip in the midsummer of 1857, while traversing Moosehead Lake in a birch (birch-bark canoe) he interrogated his Penobscot Indian guide, Joe Polis, on the point: "I asked him the meaning of the word *Musketicook*, the Indian name of Concord River. He pronounced it *Musketicook*, emphasizing the second syllable with a peculiar guttural sound, and said that it meant 'Dead-water,' which it is, and in this definition he agreed exactly with the St. Francis Indian with whom I talked in 1853."

To the experienced canoe man the word "dead-water" is a sufficient description of the character of the Concord River.

creeps through broad meadows, adorned with scattered oaks, where the cranberry is found in abundance, covering the ground like a moss-bed. A row of sunken dwarf willows borders the stream on one or both sides, while at a greater distance the meadow is skirted with maples, alders, and other fluviatile trees, overrun with the grapevine, which bears fruit in its season, purple, red, white, and other grapes. Still farther from the stream, on the edge of the firm land, are seen the gray and white dwellings of the inhabitants. According to the valuation of 1831, there were in Concord two thousand one hundred and eleven acres, or about one seventh of the whole territory, in meadow; this standing next in the list after pasturage and unimproved lands; and, judging from the returns of previous years, the meadow is not reclaimed so fast as the woods are cleared.

Let us here read what old Johnson says of these meadows in his "Wonder-Working Providence," which gives the account of New England from 1628 to 1652, and see how matters looked to him.[1] He says of the Twelfth Church of Christ gathered at Concord:

"This town is seated upon a fair fresh river, whose rivulets are filled with fresh marsh, and her streams with fish, it being a branch of that large river of Merrimack.

---

[1] *The Wonder-Working Providence of Sion's Saviour in New England,* 236 pp. was published in London in 1653 under the date of 1654 by Nathaniel Brooke at the Angel in Cornhill. This early product of the Puritan mind and the first published history of Massachusetts was the work of Captain Edward Johnson of Woburn.

Allwifes and shad in their season come up to this town, but salmon and dace cannot come up, by reason of the rocky falls, which causeth their meadows to lie much covered with water, the which these people, together with their neighbor town, have several times essayed to cut through but cannot, yet it may be turned another way with an hundred pound charge as it appeared." As to their farming he says: "Having laid out their estate upon cattle at 5 to 20 pound a cow, when they came to winter them with inland hay, and feed upon such wild fother as was never cut before, they could not hold out the winter, but, ordinarily the first or second year after their coming up to a new plantation, many of their cattle died."

And this from the same author:

"Of the Planting of the 19th Church in the Mattachusets' Government, called Sudbury:" "This year [does he mean 1654?] the town and church of Christ at Sudbury began to have the first foundation stones laid, taking up her station in the inland country, as her elder sister Concord had formerly done, lying further up the same river, being furnished with great plenty of fresh marsh, but, it lying very low is much indamaged with land floods, insomuch that when the summer proves wet they lose part of their hay; yet are they so sufficiently provided that they take in cattle of other towns to winter."

The sluggish artery of the Concord meadows steals thus unobserved through the town, without a murmur or a pulse-beat, its general course from southwest to northeast, and its length about fifty miles; a huge volume of matter, ceaselessly rolling through the plains and valleys of the substantial earth with the moccasined tread of an Indian warrior, making haste from the high places of the earth to its ancient reservoir.

The murmurs of many a famous river on the other side of the globe reach even to us here, as to more distant dwellers on its banks; many a poet's stream, floating the helms and shields of heroes on its bosom. The Xanthus or Scamander is not a mere dry channel and bed of a mountain torrent, but fed by the ever-flowing springs of fame; and I trust that I may be allowed to associate our muddy but much abused Concord River with the most famous in history.

The Mississippi, the Ganges, and the Nile, those journeying atoms from the Rocky Mountains, the Himmaleh, and Mountains of the Moon, have a kind of personal importance in the annals of the world. The heavens are not yet drained over their sources, but the Mountains of the Moon still send their annual tribute to the Pasha without

fail, as they did to the pharaohs, though he must collect the rest of his revenue at the point of the sword. Rivers must have been the guides which conducted the footsteps of the first travelers. They are the constant lure, when they flow by our doors, to distant enterprise and adventure; and, by a natural impulse, the dwellers on their banks will at length accompany their currents to the lowlands of the globe, or explore at their invitation the interior of continents. They are the natural highways of all nations, not only leveling the ground and removing obstacles from the path of the traveler, quenching his thirst and bearing him on their bosoms, but conducting him through the most interesting scenery, the most populous portions of the globe, and where the animal and vegetable kingdoms attain their greatest perfection.

I had often stood on the banks of the Concord, watching the lapse of the current, an emblem of all progress, following the same law with the system, with time, and all that is made; the weeds at the bottom gently bending down the stream, shaken by the watery wind, still planted where their seeds had sunk, but erelong to die and go down likewise; the shining pebbles, not yet anxious to better their condition, the chips and weeds, and occasional logs and stems of trees that floated past, fulfilling their fate, were objects of singular interest to me, and at last I resolved to launch myself on its bosom and float whither it would bear me.

2. Saturday

AT LENGTH, on Saturday, the last day of August, 1839, we two, brothers, and natives of Concord, weighed anchor in this river port [1]; for Concord, too, lies under the sun, a port of entry and departure for the bodies as well as the souls of men; one shore at least exempted from all duties but such as an honest man will gladly discharge. A warm, drizzling rain had obscured the morning, and threatened to delay our voyage, but at length the leaves and grass were dried, and it came out a mild afternoon, as serene

[1] John Thoreau was two years Henry's senior. They had taught school together in Concord for over a year and were reported to be in love with the same girl — Ellen Devereux Sewall. In early January of 1842, in clearing a fence, John caught his hand and wrist on a nail and tore them badly. Tetanus set in and he died on January 11th. Says Professor Canby, "Henry adored him." The dedicatory verse to *A Week on the Concord and Merrimack Rivers* reads:

> Where'er thou sail'st who sailed with me,
> Though now thou climbest loftier mounts
> And fairer rivers dost ascend,
> Be thou my Muse, my Brother ——.

and fresh as if Nature were maturing some greater scheme of her own. After this long dripping and oozing from every pore, she began to respire again more healthily than ever. So with a vigorous shove we launched our boat from the bank, while the flags and bulrushes courtesied a God-speed, and dropped silently down the stream.

Our boat, which had cost us a week's labor in the spring, was in form like a fisherman's dory, fifteen feet long by three and a half in breadth at the widest part, painted green below, with a border of blue, with reference to the two elements in which it was to spend its existence. It had been loaded the evening before at our door, half a mile from the river, with potatoes and melons from a patch which we had cultivated, and a few utensils; and was provided with wheels in order to be rolled around falls, as well as with two sets of oars, and several slender poles for shoving in shallow places, and also two masts, one of which served for a tent-pole at night; for a buffalo-skin was to be our bed, and a tent of cotton cloth our roof. It was strongly built, but heavy, and hardly of better model than usual.

If rightly made, a boat would be a sort of amphibious animal, a creature of two elements, related by one half its structure to some swift and shapely fish, and by the other to some strong-winged and graceful bird. The fish shows where there should be the greatest breadth of beam and depth in the hold; its fins direct where to set the oars, and the tail gives some hint for the form and position of the rudder. The bird shows how to rig and trim the sails, and what form to give to the prow, that it may balance the boat and divide the air and water best.

These hints we had but partially obeyed. But the eyes, though they are no sailors, will never be satisfied with any model, however fashionable, which does not answer all the requisitions of art. However, as art is all of a ship but the wood, and yet the wood alone will rudely serve the purpose of a ship, so our boat, being of wood, gladly availed itself of the old law that the heavier shall float the lighter, and though a dull water-fowl, proved a sufficient buoy for our purpose.

Some village friends stood upon a promontory lower down the stream to wave us a last farewell; but we, having already performed these shore rites, with excusable reserve, as befits those who are embarked on unusual enterprises, who behold but speak not, silently glided past the firm lands of Concord, both peopled cape and lonely summer meadow, with steady sweeps. And yet we did unbend so far as to let our guns speak for us, when at length we had swept out of sight, and thus left the woods to ring again with their echoes; and it may be many russet-clad childen, lurking in those broad meadows, with the bittern and the woodcock and the rail, though wholly concealed by brakes and hard-hack and meadow-sweet, heard our salute that afternoon.

We were soon floating past the first regular battle-ground of the Revolution, resting on our oars between the

still visible abutments of that "North Bridge," over which in April, 1775, rolled the first faint tide of that war which ceased not, till, as we read on the stone on our right, it "gave peace to these United States." As a Concord poet has sung: —[1]

[1] On the Fourth of July, 1837 at the dedication of the battle monument there was sung the Concord Hymn which had been written for the occasion by Ralph Waldo Emerson. The third stanza reveals the dedicatory purpose:

On this green bank, by this soft stream
We set today a votive stone
That memory may their dead redeem
When like our sires, our sons are gone.

The inscription on this monument reads as follows:

HERE
On the 19 of April
1775
was made
the first forcible resistance

By the rude bridge that arched the flood,
  Their flag to April's breeze unfurled,
Here once the embattled farmers stood,
  And fired the shot heard round the world.

The foe long since in silence slept;
  Alike the conqueror silent sleeps;
And Time the ruined bridge has swept
  Down the dark stream which seaward creeps.

With such thoughts we swept gently by this now peaceful pasture-ground, on waves of Concord, in which was long since drowned the din of war. That slight shaft had now sunk behind the hills, and we had floated round the neighboring bend, and under the new North Bridge between Ponkawtasset and the Poplar Hill, into the Great Meadows, which, like a broad moccasin print, have leveled a fertile and juicy place in nature.

---

to British aggression.
On the opposite Bank
stood the American Militia.
Here stood the Invading Army.
And on this spot
the first of the Enemy fell
in the War of that Revolution
which gave
Independence
to these United States.
In gratitude to GOD
and
In the love of Freedom
this Monument
was erected
AD 1836

Gradually the village murmur subsided, and we seemed to be embarked on the placid current of our dreams, floating from past to future as silently as one awakes to fresh morning or evening thoughts. We glided noiselessly down the stream, occasionally driving a pickerel or a bream from the covert of the pads, and the smaller bittern now and then sailed away on sluggish wings from some recess in the shore, or the larger lifted itself out of the long grass at our approach, and carried its precious legs away to deposit them in a place of safety. The tortoises also rapidly dropped into the water, as our boat ruffled the surface amid the willows, breaking the reflections of the trees. The banks had passed the height of their beauty, and some of the brighter flowers showed by their faded tints that the season was verging towards the afternoon of the year; but this sombre tinge enhanced their sincerity, and in the still unabated heats they seemed like the mossy brink of some cool well.

The narrow-leaved willow (*Salix Purshiana*) lay along the surface of the water in masses of light green foliage, interspersed with the large balls of the button-bush. The small rose-colored polygonum raised its head proudly above the water on either hand, and flowering at this season and in these localities, in front of dense fields of the white species which skirted the sides of the stream, its little streak of red looked very rare and precious. The pure white blossoms of the arrow-head stood in the shallower parts, and a few cardinals on the margin still

proudly surveyed themselves reflected in the water, though the latter, as well as the pickerel-weed, was now nearly out of blossom. The snake-head (*Chelone glabra*) grew close to the shore, while a kind of coreopsis, turning its brazen face to the sun, full and rank, and a tall, dull red flower (*Eupatorium purpureum,* or trumpet-weed) formed the rear rank of the fluvial array. The bright blue flowers of the soapwort gentian were sprinkled here and there in the adjacent meadows, like flowers which Proserpine had dropped, and still farther in the fields or higher on the bank were seen the purple Gerardia, the Virginian rhexia, and drooping neottia or ladies'-tresses; while from the more distant waysides which we occasionally passed, and banks where the sun had lodged, was reflected still a dull yellow beam from the ranks of tansy, now past its prime.

In short, Nature seemed to have adorned herself for our departure with a profusion of fringes and curls, mingled with the bright tints of flowers, reflected in the water. But we missed the white water-lily, which is the queen of river flowers, its reign being over for this season. He makes his voyage too late, perhaps, by a true water clock who delays so long. Many of this species inhabit our Concord water. I have passed down the river before sunrise on a summer morning, between fields of lilies still shut in sleep; and when, at length, the flakes of sunlight from over the bank fell on the surface of the water, whole fields of white blossoms seemed to flash open before me, as I floated along, like the unfolding of a banner, so sensible is this flower to the influence of the sun's rays.

As we were floating through the last of these familiar meadows, we observed the large and conspicuous flowers of the hibiscus, covering the dwarf willows and mingled with the leaves of the grape, and wished that we could inform one of our friends behind of the locality of this somewhat rare and inaccessible flower before it was too late to pluck it; but we were just gliding out of sight of the village spire before it occurred to us that the farmer in the adjacent meadow would go to church on the morrow, and would carry this news for us; and so by the Monday, while we should be floating on the Merrimack, our friend would be reaching to pluck this blossom on the bank of the Concord.

After a pause at Ball's Hill, the St. Ann's of Concord voyageurs, not to say any prayer for the success of our voyage, but to gather the few berries which were still left on the hills, hanging by very slender threads, we weighed anchor again, and were soon out of sight of our native village. The land seemed to grow fairer as we withdrew from it. Far away to the southwest lay the quiet village, left alone under its elms and buttonwoods in mid-afternoon; and the hills, notwithstanding their blue, ethereal faces, seemed to cast a saddened eye on their old playfellows; but, turning short to the north, we bade adieu to their familiar outlines, and addressed ourselves to new scenes and adventures. Naught was familiar but the heavens, from under whose roof the voyageur never passes; but with their countenance, and the acquaintance we had with river and wood, we trusted to fare well under any circumstances.

From this point the river runs perfectly straight for a mile or more to Carlisle Bridge, which consists of twenty wooden piers, and when we looked back over it, its surface was reduced to a line's breadth and appeared like a cobweb gleaming in the sun.[1] Here and there might be seen a pole sticking up, to mark the place where some fisherman had enjoyed unusual luck, and in return had consecrated his rod to the deities who preside over these shallows. It was full twice as broad as before, deep and tranquil, with a muddy bottom, and bordered with willows, beyond which spread broad lagoons covered with pads, bulrushes, and flags.

Late in the afternoon we passed a man on the shore fishing with a long birch pole, its silvery bark left on, and a dog at his side, rowing so near as to agitate his cork

---

[1] Seen from a distance this reach later evoked the following passage (October 6, 1851):

"The reach of the river between Bedford and Carlisle, seen from a distance in the road today, as formerly has a singularly ethereal, celestial, or elysian look. It is of a light sky-blue, alternating with smoother white streaks, where the surface reflects the light differently, like a milk-pan full of the milk of Valhalla partially skimmed, more gloriously and heavenly fair and pure than the sky itself. It is something more celestial than the sky above it. I never saw any water look so celestial. I have often noticed it."

The courtesy of Houghton Mifflin Company is acknowledged in relation to this and other passages from the Journal appearing in these notes.

with our oars, and drive away luck for a season; and when we had rowed a mile as straight as an arrow, with our faces turned towards him, and the bubbles in our wake still visible on the tranquil surface, there stood the fisher still with his dog, like statues under the other side of the heavens, the only objects to relieve the eye in the extended meadow; and there would he stand abiding his luck, till he took his way home through the fields at evening with his fish. Thus, by one bait or another, Nature allures inhabitants into all her recesses. This man was the last of our townsmen whom we saw, and we silently through him bade adieu to our friends.

The characteristics and pursuits of various ages and races of men are always existing in epitome in every neighborhood. The pleasures of my earliest youth have become the inheritance of other men. This man is still a fisher, and belongs to an era in which I myself have lived. Perchance he is not confounded by many knowledges, and has not sought out many inventions, but how to take many fishes before the sun sets, with his slender birchen pole and flaxen line, that is invention enough for him. It is good even to be a fisherman in summer and in winter.

Some men are judges, these August days, sitting on benches, even till the court rises; they sit judging there honorably, between the seasons and between meals, leading a civil politic life, arbitrating in the case of Spaulding *versus* Cummings, it may be, from highest noon till the red vesper sinks into the west. The fisherman, meanwhile, stands in three feet of water, under the same summer's sun, arbitrating in other cases between muckworm and shiner, amid the fragrance of water-lilies, mint, and pontederia, leading his life many rods from dry land, within a pole's length of where the larger fishes swim. Human life is to him very much like a river, "renning aie downward to the sea." This was his observation. His honor made a great discovery in bailments.

I can just remember an old brown-coated man who was the Walton of this stream, who had come over from Newcastle, England, with his son,—the latter a stout and hearty man who had lifted an anchor in his day. A straight old man he was, who took his way in silence through the meadows, having passed the period of communication with his fellows; his old experienced coat, hanging long and straight and brown as the yellow-pine bark, glittering with so much smothered sunlight, if you stood near enough, no work of art but naturalized at length. I often discovered him unexpectedly amid the pads and the gray willows when he moved, fishing in some old country method,—for youth and age then went a-fishing together,—full of incommunicable thoughts, perchance about his own Tyne and Northumberland.

He was always to be seen in serene afternoons haunting the river, and almost rustling with the sedge; so many sunny hours in an old man's life, entrapping silly fish; almost grown to be the sun's familiar; what need had he of hat or raiment any, having served out his time, and seen through such thin disguises? I have seen how his coeval fates rewarded him with the yellow perch, and yet I thought his luck was not in proportion to his years; and I have seen when, with slow steps and weighed down with aged thoughts, he disappeared with his fish under his low-roofed house on the skirts of the village. I think nobody else saw him; nobody else remembers him now, for he soon after died, and migrated to new Tyne streams. His fishing was not a sport, nor solely a means of subsistence, but a sort of solemn sacrament and withdrawal from the world, just as the aged read their Bibles.

Whether we live by the seaside, or by the lakes and rivers, or on the prairie, it concerns us to attend to the nature of fishes, since they are not phenomena confined to certain localities only, but forms and phases of the life in nature universally dispersed. The countless shoals which annually coast the shores of Europe and America are not so interesting to the student of nature as the more fertile law itself, which deposits their spawn on the tops of mountains and on the interior plains; the fish principle in nature, from which it results that they may be found in water in so many places, in greater or less numbers. The natural historian is not a fisherman who prays for cloudy days and good luck merely; but as fishing has been styled "a contemplative man's recreation," introducing him profitably to woods and water, so the fruit of the naturalist's observations is not in new genera or species, but in new contemplations still, and science is only a more contemplative man's recreation.

The seeds of the life of fishes are everywhere disseminated, whether the winds waft them, or the waters float them, or the deep earth holds them; wherever a pond is dug, straightway it is stocked with this vivacious race. They have a lease of nature, and it is not yet out. The Chinese are bribed to carry their ova from province to province in jars or in hollow reeds, or the water-birds to transport them to the mountain tarns and interior lakes. There are fishes wherever there is a fluid medium, and even in clouds and in melted metals we detect their semblance. Think how in winter you can sink a line down straight in a pasture through snow and through ice, and pull up a bright, slippery, dumb subterranean silver or golden fish! It is curious, also, to reflect how they make one family, from the largest to the smallest. The least minnow that lies on the ice as bait for pickerel looks like a huge seafish cast up on the shore.

In the waters of this town there are about a dozen distinct species, though the inexperienced would expect many more.[1] It enhances our sense of the grand security

[1] On July 20, 1851 Thoreau recorded in his *Journal*:

"The river, too, steadily yields its crop. In louring days it is remarkable how many villagers resort to it. It is of more worth than many gardens. I meet one, late in the afternoon, going to the river with his basket on his arm and his pole in hand, not ambitious to catch pickerel this time, but he thinks he may perhaps get a mess of small fish. These [*sic*] kind of values are real and important, though but little appreciated,

and serenity of nature to observe the still undisturbed economy and content of the fishes of this century, their happiness a regular fruit of the summer.

The fresh-water sun-fish, bream, or ruff (*Pomotis vulgaris*), as it were, without ancestry, without posterity, still represents the fresh-water sun-fish in nature. It is the most common of all, and seen on every urchin's string; a simple and inoffensive fish, whose nests are visible all along the shore, hollowed in the sand, over which it is steadily poised through the summer hours on waving fin.

---

and he is not a wise legislator who underrates them and allows the bridges to be built low so as to prevent the passage of small boats. The town is but little conscious how much interest it has in the river, and might vote it away any day thoughtlessly. There is always to be seen either some unshaven wading man, an old mower of the river meadows, familiar with water, vibrating his long pole over the lagoons of the off-shore pads, or else some solitary fisher, in a boat behind the willows, like a mote in the sunbeams reflecting the light; and who can tell how many a mess of river fish is daily cooked in the town? They are an important article of food to many a poor family."

Sometimes there are twenty or thirty nests in the space of a few rods, two feet wide by half a foot in depth, and made with no little labor, the weeds being removed, and the sand shoved up on the sides, like a bowl.

Here it may be seen early in summer assiduously brooding, and driving away minnows and larger fishes, even its own species, which would disturb its ova, pursuing them a few feet, and circling round swiftly to its nest again; the minnows, like young sharks, instantly entering the empty nests, meanwhile, and swallowing the spawn, which is attached to the weeds and to the bottom, on the sunny side. The spawn is exposed to so many dangers that a very small proportion can ever become fishes, for beside being the constant prey of birds and fishes, a great many nests are made so near the shore, in shallow water, that they are left dry in a few days, as the river goes down. These and the lamprey's are the only fishes' nests that I have observed, though the ova of some species may be seen floating on the surface.

The breams are so careful of their charge that you may stand close by in the water and examine them at your leisure. I have thus stood over them half an hour at a time, and stroked them familiarly without frightening them, suffering them to nibble my fingers harmlessly, and seen them erect their dorsal fins in anger when my hand approached their ova, and have even taken them gently out of the water with my hand; though this cannot be accomplished by a sudden movement, however dexterous, for instant warning is conveyed to them through their denser element, but only by letting the fingers gradually close about them as they are poised over the palm, and with the utmost gentleness raising them slowly to the surface. Though stationary, they kept up a constant sculling or waving motion with their fins, which is exceedingly graceful, and expressive of their humble happiness; for unlike ours, the element in which they live is a stream which must be constantly resisted.

From time to time they nibble the weeds at the bottom or overhanging their nests, or dart after a fly or a worm. The dorsal fin, besides answering the purpose of a keel, with the anal, serves to keep the fish upright, for in shallow water, where this is not covered, they fall on their sides. As you stand thus stooping over the bream in its nest, the edges of the dorsal and caudal fins have a singular dusty golden reflection, and its eyes, which stand out from the head, are transparent and colorless.

Seen in its native element, it is a very beautiful and compact fish, perfect in all its parts, and looks like a brilliant coin fresh from the mint. It is a perfect jewel of the river, the green, red, coppery, and golden reflections of its mottled sides being the concentration of such rays as struggle through the floating pads and flowers to the sandy bottom, and in harmony with the sunlit brown and yellow pebbles. Behind its watery shield it dwells far from many accidents inevitable to human life.

There is also another species of bream found in our

river, without the red spot on the operculum, which, according to M. Agassiz, is undescribed.

The common perch (*Perca flavescens*), which name describes well the gleaming, golden reflections of its scales as it is drawn out of the water, its red gills standing out in vain in the thin element, is one of the handsomest and most regularly formed of our fishes, and at such a moment as this reminds us of the fish in the picture which wished to be restored to its native element until it had grown larger; and indeed most of this species that are caught are not half grown. In the ponds there is a light-colored and slender kind, which swim in shoals of many hundreds in the sunny water, in company with the shiner, averaging not more than six or seven inches in length, while only a few larger specimens are found in the deepest water, which prey upon their weaker brethren.

I have often attracted these small perch to the shore at evening, by rippling the water with my fingers, and they may sometimes be caught while attempting to pass inside your hands. It is a tough and heedless fish, biting from impulse, without nibbling, and from impulse refraining to bite, and sculling indifferently past. It rather prefers the clear water and sandy bottoms, though here it has not much choice. It is a true fish, such as the angler loves to put into his basket or hang at the top of his willow twig, in shady afternoons along the banks of the stream. So many unquestionable fishes he counts, and so many shiners, which he counts and then throws away.

Old Josselyn in his *New England's Rarities,* published in 1672, mentions the Perch or River Partridge.[1]

The chivin, dace, roach, cousin trout, or whatever else it is called (*Leuciscus pulchellus*), white and red, is always an unexpected prize, which, however, any angler is glad to hook for its rarity; — a name that reminds us of many an unsuccessful ramble by swift streams, when the wind rose to disappoint the fisher. It is commonly a silvery soft-scaled fish, of graceful, scholarlike, and classical look, like many a picture in an English book. It loves a swift current and a sandy bottom, and bites inadvertently, yet not without appetite for the bait. The minnows are used as bait for pickerel in the winter. The red chivin, according to some, is still the same fish, only older, or with its tints deepened as they think by the darker water it inhabits, as the red clouds swim in the twilight atmosphere.

He who has not hooked the red chivin is not yet a complete angler. Other fishes, methinks, are slightly amphibious, but this is a denizen of the water wholly. The cork goes dancing down the swift-rushing stream, amid the weeds and sands, when suddenly, by a coincidence never to be remembered, emerges this fabulous inhabitant of another element, a thing heard of but not seen, as if it were the instant creation of an eddy, a true product of the running stream. And this bright cupreous dolphin

---

[1] *New England's Rarities,* John Josselyn, Gent., London, 1672, page 28.

was spawned and has passed its life beneath the level of your feet in your native fields. Fishes too, as well as birds and clouds, derive their armor from the mine. I have heard of mackerel visiting the copper banks at a particular season; this fish, perchance, has its habitat in the Coppermine River. I have caught white chivin of great size in the Aboljacknagesic, where it empties into the Penobscot, at the base of Mount Ktaadn, but no red ones there.[1]

---

[1] The occasion had been the evening before Thoreau's ascent of Mount Ktaadn [Katahdin] in early September, 1846:

"We had been told by McCauslin that we should here find trout enough; so, while some prepared the camp, the rest fell to fishing. Seizing the birch poles which some party of Indians, or white hunters, had left on the shore, and baiting our hooks with pork, and with trout, as soon as they were caught, we cast our lines into the mouth of the Aboljacknagesic, a clear, swift, shallow stream, which came in from Ktaadn. Instantly a shoal of white chivin (*Leucisci pulchelli*), silvery roaches, cousin-trout, or what not, large and small, prowling thereabouts, fell upon our bait, and one after another were landed amidst the bushes. Anon their cousins, the true trout, took their turn, and alternately the speckled trout, and the silvery roaches, swallowed the bait as fast as we could throw in; and the finest specimens of both that I have ever seen, the largest one weighing three pounds, were heaved upon the shore, though at first in vain, to wriggle down into the water again, for we stood in the boat; but soon we learned to remedy this evil; for one, who had lost his hook, stood on shore to catch them as they fell in a perfect shower around him, — sometimes, wet and slippery, full in his face and bosom, as his arms were outstretched to receive them.

"While yet alive, before their tints had faded, they glistened like the fairest flowers, the product of primitive rivers; and he could hardly trust his senses, as he stood over them, that these jewels should have swam away in that Aboljacknagesic water for so long, so many dark ages; — these bright fluviatile flowers, seen of Indians only, made beautiful, the Lord only knows why, to swim there! . . .

"In the night I dreamed of trout-fishing; and, when at length I awoke, it seemed a fable that this painted fish swam there so near my couch, and rose to our hooks the last evening, and I doubted if I had not dreamed it all. So I arose before dawn to test its truth, while my companions were still sleeping. There stood Ktaadn with distinct and cloud-

The latter variety seems not to have been sufficiently observed.

The dace (*Leuciscus argenteus*) is a slight silvery minnow, found generally in the middle of the stream where the current is most rapid, and frequently confounded with the last named.

The shiner (*Leuciscus chrysoleucus*) is a soft-scaled and tender fish, the victim of its stronger neighbors, found in all places, deep and shallow, clear and turbid; generally the first nibbler at the bait, but, with its small mouth and nibbling propensities, not easily caught. It is a gold or silver bit that passes current in the river, its limber tail

less outline in the moonlight; and the rippling of the rapids was the only sound to break the stillness. Standing on the shore, I once more cast my line into the stream, and found the dream to be real and the fable true. The speckled trout and silvery roach, like flying-fish, sped swiftly through the moonlight air, describing bright arcs on the dark side of Ktaadn, until moonlight, now fading into daylight, brought satiety to my mind, and the minds of my companions who had joined me." *The Maine Woods,* N.Y. 1950.

dimpling the surface in sport or flight. I have seen the fry, when frightened by something thrown into the water, leap out by dozens, together with the dace, and wreck themselves upon a floating plank. It is the little light-infant of the river, with body armor of gold or silver spangles, slipping, gliding its life through with a quirk of the tail, half in the water, half in the air, upward and ever upward with flitting fin to more crystalline tides, yet still abreast of us dwellers on the bank. It is almost dissolved by the summer heats. A slighter and lighter colored shiner is found in one of our ponds.

The pickerel (*Esox reticulatus*), the swiftest, wariest, and most ravenous of fishes, which Josselyn calls the fresh-water or river wolf, is very common in the shallow and weedy lagoons along the sides of the stream. It is a solemn, stately, ruminant fish, lurking under the shadow of a pad at noon, with still, circumspect, voracious eye, motionless as a jewel set in water, or moving slowly along to take up its position, darting from time to time at such unlucky fish or frog or insect as comes within its range, and swallowing it at a gulp. I have caught one which had swallowed a brother pickerel half as large as itself, with the tail still visible in its mouth, while the head was aleady digested in its stomach. Sometimes a striped snake, bound to greener meadows across the stream, ends its undulatory progress in the same receptacle. They are so greedy and impetuous that they are frequently caught by being entangled in the line the moment it is cast.

Fishermen also distinguish the brook pickerel, a shorter and thicker fish than the former.

The horned pout (*Pimelodus nebulosus*), sometimes called Minister, from the peculiar squeaking noise it makes when drawn out of the water, is a dull and blundering fellow, and, like the eel, vespertinal in his habits and fond of the mud. It bites deliberately, as if about its business. They are taken at night with a mass of worms strung on a thread, which catches in their teeth, sometimes three or four, with an eel, at one pull. They are extremely tenacious of life, opening and shutting their mouths for half an hour after their heads have been cut off; a bloodthirsty and bullying race of rangers, inhabiting the fertile river bottoms, with ever a lance in rest, and ready to do battle with their nearest neighbor. I have observed them in summer, when every other one had a long and bloody scar upon his back, where the skin was gone, the mark, perhaps, of some fierce encounter. Sometimes the fry, not an inch long, are seen darkening the shore with their myriads.

The suckers (*Catostomi Bostonienses* and *tuberculati*), common and horned, perhaps on an average the largest of our fishes, may be seen in shoals of a hundred or more, stemming the current in the sun, on their mysterious migrations, and sometimes sucking in the bait which the fisherman suffers to float toward them. The former, which sometimes grow to a large size, are frequently caught by the hand in the brooks, or like the red chivin are jerked out by a hook fastened firmly to the end of a stick, and placed under their jaws. They are hardly known to the mere angler, however, not often biting at his baits, though the spearer carries home many a mess in the spring. To our village eyes, these shoals have a foreign and imposing aspect, realizing the fertility of the seas.

The common eel, too (*Murœna Bostoniensis*), the only species of eel known in the State, a slimy, squirming creature, informed of mud, still squirming in the pan, is speared and hooked up with various success. Methinks it too occurs in picture, left after the deluge, in many a meadow high and dry.

In the shallow parts of the river where the current is rapid and the bottom pebbly, you may sometimes see the curious circular nests of the lamprey eel (*Petromyzon Americanus*), the American stone-sucker, as large as a cartwheel, a foot or two in height, and sometimes rising half a foot above the surface of the water. They collect these stones, of the size of a hen's egg, with their mouths, as their name implies, and are said to fashion them into circles with their tails. They ascend falls by clinging to the stones, which may sometimes be raised by lifting the fish by the tail. As they are not seen on their way down the streams, it is thought by fishermen that they never return, but waste away and die, clinging to rocks and stumps of trees for an indefinite period; a tragic feature in the scenery of the river bottoms worthy to be remembered with Shakespeare's description of the sea-floor. They are rarely seen in our waters at present, on account of the dams, though they are taken in great quantities at the mouth of the river in Lowell. Their nests, which are very conspicuous, look more like art than anything in the river.

If we had leisure this afternoon, we might turn our prow up the brooks in quest of the classical trout and the minnows. Of the last alone, according to M. Agassiz, several of the species found in this town are yet undescribed. These would, perhaps, complete the list of our finny contemporaries in the Concord waters.

Salmon, shad, and alewives were formerly abundant here, and taken in weirs by the Indians, who taught this method to the whites, by whom they were used as food and as manure, until the dam and afterward the canal at Billerica, and the factories at Lowell, put an end to their migrations hitherward; though it is thought that a few more enterprising shad may still occasionally be seen in this part of the river. It is said, to account for the destruction of the fishery, that those who at that time represented the interests of the fishermen and the fishes, remembering between what dates they were accustomed to take the grown shad, stipulated that the dams should be left open for that season only, and the fry, which go down a month later, were consequently stopped and destroyed by myriads. Others say that the fish-ways were not properly constructed. Perchance, after a few thousands of years, if the fishes will be patient, and pass their summers elsewhere meanwhile, nature will have leveled the Billerica dam, and the Lowell factories, and the Grass-ground River run clear again, to be explored by new migratory shoals, even as far as the Hopkinton pond and Westborough swamp.

One would like to know more of that race, now extinct, whose seines lie rotting in the garrets of their children, who openly professed the trade of fishermen, and even fed their townsmen creditably, not skulking through the meadows to a rainy afternoon sport. Dim visions we still get of miraculous draughts of fishes, and heaps uncountable by the river-side, from the tales of our seniors sent on horseback in their childhood from the neighboring towns, perched on saddlebags, with instructions to get the one bag filled with shad, the other with alewives.

At least one momento of those days may still exist in the memory of this generation, in the familiar appellation of a celebrated train-band of this town, whose untrained ancestors stood creditably at Concord North Bridge. Their captain, a man of piscatory tastes, having duly warned his company to turn out on a certain day, they, like obedient soldiers, appeared promptly on parade at the appointed time, but, unfortunately, they went undrilled, except in the manœuvres of a soldier's wit and unlicensed jesting, that May day; for their captain, forgetting his own appointment, and warned only by the favorable aspect of the heavens, as he had often done before, went a-fishing that afternoon, and his company thenceforth was known to old and young, grave and gay, as "The Shad," and by the youths of this vicinity this was long regarded as the proper name of all the irregular militia in Christendom.

But, alas! no record of these fishers' lives remain that we know, unless it be one brief page of hard but unquestionable history, which occurs in Day Book No. 4, of an old trader of this town, long since dead, which shows pretty plainly what constituted a fisherman's stock in trade in those days. It purports to be a Fisherman's Account Current, probably for the fishing season of the year 1805, during which months he purchased daily rum and sugar, sugar and rum, N. E. and W. I., "one cod line," "one brown mug," and "a line for the seine;" rum and sugar, sugar and rum, "good loaf sugar," and "good brown," W. I. and N. E., in short and uniform entries to the bottom of the page, all carried out in pounds, shilling, and pence, from March 25 to June 5, and promptly settled by receiving "cash in full" at the last date.[1] But perhaps not so settled altogether.

[1] The capitals N. E. and W. I. represent, respectively, the varieties of rum then known as New England and West India. The entire account is given on page 474 of Volume 1 of the Journal, as follows:

Fisherman's Acct. for 1805 Began March 25

		cts.
	Dd Mr. Sam Potter 2 qts W I 3/ 1 lb. sugar 10d	$0.64
	One Cod line 5/	84
April	8 Qt W I 1/6 & 1 lb Sugar 10d & Brown Mug	48
	9 Qt N E rum 1/ 10th Do. of Do 1/	33
	13 Qt N E rum & lb Sugar 15th 2 Qts N E rum 2/	62
	17 Qt W I 1/6 Do N E 1/lb Sugar 9d & Qt N E Rum	71
	22 Qt N E rum 1/lb sugar 9d & Qt N E rum 1/	44½
	23 Qt N E rum 1/ Do of Do & sugar 5d	39

These were the necessaries of life in those days; with salmon, shad, and alewives, fresh and pickled, he was thereafter independent on the groceries. Rather a preponderance of the fluid elements; but such is the fisherman's nature. I can faintly remember to have seen this same fisher in my earliest youth, still as near the river as he could get, with uncertain, undulatory step, after so many things had gone downstream, swinging a scythe in the meadow, his bottle like a serpent hid in the grass; himself as yet not cut down by the Great Mower.

Shad are still taken in the basin of Concord River, at Lowell, where they are said to be a month earlier than the Merrimack shad, on account of the warmth of the water. Still patiently, almost pathetically, with instinct not to be discouraged, not to be *reasoned* with, revisiting their old haunts, as if their stern fates would relent, and still met by the Corporation with its dam. Poor shad! where is thy redress? When Nature gave thee instinct, gave she thee the heart to bear thy fate? Still wandering

---

24	Qt N E rum 1/lb sugar 9d	28½
29	Qt N E rum 1/ & lb sugar 9d — 30th Rum 1/	44½
May first	Qt rum ½ lb Sugar 1/5d	22
	Qt N E rum 1/ & ½ lb Loaf Sugar 9d	29
4	Qt rum 1/ Sugar 5d	22
6	Qt N E rum 1/ & lb good sugar 11d	31
7	Qt N E rum 1/8th Qt N E rum 1/ & ½ lb Sugar 5d	40
11	Qt N E rum 11d lb Sugar 10d	29
15	Qt rum & lb Sugar 1/9 & Qt N E rum	44
16	To a Line for the Sceene 3/	0.50
20	To Qt N E rum 11d lb Sugar 10d	0.29
21	To Qt N E rum 11d & lb Sugar 10d	0.29
27	To Qt W I 1/6 & lb Sugar 10d	0.39
June 5th 1805	Settled this acct by Recev.g Cash in Full	$8.82½

the sea in thy scaly armor to inquire humbly at the mouths of rivers if man has perchance left them free for thee to enter. By countless shoals loitering uncertain meanwhile, merely stemming the tide there, in danger from sea foes in spite of thy bright armor, awaiting new instructions, until the sands, until the water itself, tell thee if it be so or not.

Thus by whole migrating nations, full of instinct, which is thy faith, in this backward spring, turned adrift, and perchance knowest not where men do *not* dwell, where there are *not* factories, in these days. Armed with no sword, no electric shock, but mere shad, armed only with innocence and a just cause, with tender dumb mouth only forward, and scales easy to be detached. I for one am with thee, and who knows what may avail a crow-bar against that Billerica dam? — Not despairing when whole myriads have gone to feed those sea monsters during thy suspense, but still brave, indifferent, on easy fin there, like shad reserved for higher destinies. Willing to be decimated for man's behoof after the spawning season.

Away with the superficial and selfish phil-*anthropy* of men, — who knows what admirable virtue of fishes may be below low-water-mark, bearing up against a hard destiny, not admired by that fellow-creature who alone can appreciate it! Who hears the fishes when they cry? It will not be forgotten by some memory that we were contemporaries. Thou shalt erelong have thy way up the rivers, up all the rivers of the globe, if I am not mistaken. Yea, even thy dull watery dream shall be more than realized. If it were not so, but thou wert to be overlooked at first and at last, then would not I take their heaven. Yes, I say so, who think I know better than thou canst. Keep a stiff fin, then, and stem all the tides thou mayst meet.

At length it would seem that the interests, not of the fishes only, but of the men of Wayland, of Sudbury, of Concord, demand the leveling of that dam. Innumerable acres of meadow are waiting to be made dry land, wild native grass to give place to English. The farmers stand with scythes whet, waiting the subsiding of the waters, by gravitation, by evaporation, or otherwise, but sometimes their eyes do not rest, their wheels do not roll, on the quaking meadow ground during the haying season at all. So many sources of wealth inaccessible. They rate the loss hereby incurred in the single town of Wayland alone as equal to the expense of keeping a hundred yoke of oxen the year round.

One year, as I learn, not long ago, the farmers standing ready to drive their teams afield as usual, the water gave no signs of falling; without new attraction in the heavens, without freshet or visible cause, still standing stagnant at an unprecedented height. All hydrometers were at fault; some trembled for their English, even. But speedy emissaries revealed the unnatural secret, in the new float-board, wholly a foot in width, added to their already too high privileges by the dam proprietors. The hundred yoke of oxen, meanwhile, standing patient, gazing wishfully meadowward, at that inaccessible waving native grass, uncut but by the great mower Time, who cuts so broad a swathe, without so much as a wisp to wind about their horns.

That was a long pull from Ball's Hill to Carlisle Bridge, sitting with our faces to the south, a slight breeze rising from the north; but nevertheless water still runs and grass grows, for now, having passed the bridge between Carlisle and Bedford, we see men haying far off in the meadow, their heads waving like the grass which they cut. In the distance the wind seemed to bend all alike. As the night stole over, such a freshness was wafted across the meadow that every blade of cut grass seemed to teem with life. Faint purple clouds began to be reflected in the water, and the cow-bells tinkled louder along the banks, while, like sly water-rats, we stole along nearer the shore, looking for a place to pitch our camp.

At length, when we had made about seven miles, as far as Billerica, we moored our boat on the west side of a little rising ground which in the spring forms an island in the river. Here we found huckleberries still hanging upon the bushes, where they seemed to have slowly ripened for our especial use. Bread and sugar, and cocoa boiled in river water, made our repast, and as we had drank in the fluvial prospect all day, so now we took a draft of the water with our evening meal to propitiate the river gods, and whet our vision for the sights it was to behold. The sun was setting on the one hand, while our eminence was contributing its shadow to the night on the other. It seemed insensibly to grow lighter as the night shut in, and a distant and solitary farm-house was revealed, which before lurked in the shadows of the noon.

There was no other house in sight, nor any cultivated field. To the right and left, as far as the horizon, were straggling pine woods with their plumes against the sky, and across the river were rugged hills, covered with shrub oaks, tangled with grape-vines and ivy, with here and there a gray rock jutting out from the maze. The sides of these cliffs, though a quarter of a mile distant, were almost heard to rustle while we looked at them, it was such a leafy wilderness; a place for fauns and satyrs, and where bats hung all day to the rocks, and at evening flitted over the water, and fire-flies husbanded their light under the grass and leaves against the night.

When we had pitched our tent on the hillside, a few rods from the shore, we sat looking through its triangular door in the twilight at our lonely mast on the shore just seen above the alders, and hardly yet come to a standstill from the swaying of the stream; the first encroachment of commerce on this land. There was our port, our Ostia. That straight, geometrical line against the water and the sky stood for the last refinements of civilized life, and what of sublimity there is in history was there symbolized.

For the most part, there was no recognition of human

life in the night, no human breathing was heard, only the breathing of the wind. As we sat up, kept awake by the novelty of our situation, we heard at intervals foxes stepping about over the dead leaves, and brushing the dewy grass close to our tent, and once a musquash fumbling among the potatoes and melons in our boat; but when we hastened to the shore we could detect only a ripple in the water ruffling the disk of a star. At intervals we were serenaded by the song of a dreaming sparrow or the throttled cry of an owl; but after each sound which near at hand broke the stillness of the night, each crackling of the twigs, or rustling among the leaves, there was a sudden pause, and deeper and more conscious silence, as if the intruder were aware that no life was rightfully abroad at that hour.

There was a fire in Lowell, as we judged, this night, and we saw the horizon blazing, and heard the distant alarmbells, as it were a faint tinkling music borne to these woods.[1] But the most constant and memorable sound of a summer's night, which we did not fail to hear every night afterward, though at no time so incessantly and so favorably as now, was the barking of the house-dogs, from the loudest and hoarsest bark to the faintest aerial palpitation under the eaves of heaven, from the patient but anxious mastiff to the timid and wakeful terrier, at first loud and rapid, then faint and slow, to be imitated only in a whisper; wow-wow-wow-wow—wo—wo—w—w. Even in a retired and uninhabited district like this, it was a sufficiency of sound for the ear of night, and more impressive than any music.

I have heard the voice of a hound, just before daylight, while the stars were shining, from over the woods and river, far in the horizon, when it sounded as sweet and melodious as an instrument. The hounding of a dog pursuing a fox or other animal in the horizon may have first suggested the notes of the hunting-horn to alternate with and relieve the lungs of the dog. This natural bugle long resounded in the woods of the ancient world before the horn was invented. The very dogs that sullenly bay the moon from farm-yards in these nights excite more heroism in our breasts than all the civil exhortations or war sermons of the age. "I would rather be a dog, and bay the moon," than many a Roman that I know.

The night is equally indebted to the clarion of the cock,

---

[1] A search in the files of the Lowell newspapers of the time, the *Courier* and the *Advertiser*, has failed to reveal any reference to this fire.

with wakeful hope, from the very setting of the sun, prematurely ushering in the dawn. All these sounds, the crowing of cocks, the baying of dogs, and the hum of insects at noon, are the evidence of nature's health or *sound* state. Such is the never-failing beauty and accuracy of language, the most perfect art in the world; the chisel of a thousand years retouches it.

At length the antepenultimate and drowsy hours drew on, and all sounds were denied entrance to our ears.

3. *Sunday*

In the morning the river and adjacent country were covered with a dense fog, through which the smoke of our fire curled up like a still subtiler mist; but before we had rowed many rods, the sun arose and the fog rapidly dispersed, leaving a slight steam only to curl along the surface of the water. It was a quiet Sunday morning, with more of the auroral rosy and white than of the yellow light in it, as if it dated from earlier than the fall of man, and still preserved a heathenish integrity.

But the impressions which the morning makes vanish with its dews, and not even the most "persevering mortal" can preserve the memory of its freshness to midday. As we passed the various islands, or what were islands in the spring, rowing with our backs downstream, we gave names to them. The one on which we had camped we called Fox Island, and one fine densely wooded island surounded by deep water and overrun by grape-vines, which looked like a mass of verdure and of flowers cast upon the waves, we named Grape Island. From Ball's Hill to Billerica meeting-house, the river was still twice as broad as in Concord, a deep, dark, and dead stream, flowing between gentle hills and sometimes cliffs, and well wooded all the way. It was a long woodland lake bordered with willows. For long reaches we could see neither house nor cultivated field, nor any sign of the vicinity of man. Now we coasted along some shallow shore by the edge of a dense palisade of bulrushes, which straightly bounded the water as if clipped by art, reminding us of the reed forts of the East-Indians of which we had read; and now the bank, slightly raised, was overhung with graceful grasses and various species of brake, whose downy stems stood closely grouped and naked as in a vase, while their heads spread several feet on either side.

The dead limbs of the willow were rounded and adorned by the climbing mikania (*Mikania scandens*), which filled every crevice in the leafy bank, contrasting agreeably with the gray bark of its supporter and the balls of the button-bush. The water willow (*Salix Purshiana*), when it is of large size and entire, is the most graceful and ethereal of our trees. Its masses of light-green foliage, piled one upon another to the height of twenty or thirty feet, seemed to float on the surface of the water, while the slight gray stems and the shore were hardly visible between them. No tree is so wedded to the water, and harmonizes so well with still streams. It is even more graceful than the weeping willow, or any pendulous trees which dip their branches in the stream instead of being buoyed up by it. Its limbs curved outward over the surface as if attracted by it. It had not a New England but an Oriental character, reminding us of trim Persian gardens, of Haroun Alraschid, and the artificial lakes of the East.

As we thus dipped our way along between fresh masses of foliage overrun with the grape and smaller flowering vines, the surface was so calm, and both air and water so transparent, that the flight of a kingfisher or robin over the river was as distinctly seen reflected in the water below as in the air above. The birds seemed to flit through submerged groves, alighting on the yielding sprays, and their clear notes to come up from below. We were uncertain whether the water floated the land, or the land held the water in its bosom. It was such a season, in short, as that in which one of our Concord poets sailed on its stream, and sung its quiet glories.

For every oak and birch, too, growing on the hill-top, as well as for these elms and willows, we knew that there was a graceful ethereal and ideal tree making down from the roots, and sometimes Nature in high tides brings her mirror to its foot and makes it visible. The stillness was intense and almost conscious, as if it were a natural Sabbath, and we fancied that the morning was the evening of a celestial day. The air was so elastic and crystalline that it had the same effect on the landscape that a glass has on a picture, to give it an ideal remoteness and perfection. The landscape was clothed in a mild and quiet light, in which the woods and fences checkered and partitioned it with new regularity, and rough and uneven fields stretched away with lawn-like smoothness to the horizon, and the clouds, finely distinct and picturesque, seemed a fit drapery to hang over fairy-land. The world seemed decked for some holiday or prouder pageantry, with silken streamers flying, and the course of our lives to wind on before us like a green lane into a country maze, at the season when fruit-trees are in blossom.

Why should not our whole life and its scenery be actually thus fair and distinct? All our lives want a suitable background. They should at least, like the life of the anchorite, be as impressive to behold as objects in the desert, a broken shaft or crumbling mound against a limitless horizon. Character always secures for itself this advantage, and is thus distinct and unrelated to near or trivial objects, whether things or persons. On this same stream a maiden once sailed in my boat, thus unattended but by invisible guardians, and as she sat in the prow there was nothing but herself between the steersman and the sky.[1] At evening, still the very stars seem but this maiden's emissaries and reporters of her progress.

It required some rudeness to disturb with our boat the mirror-like surface of the water, in which every twig and

[1] This passage is believed to refer to Ellen Devereux Sewall, with whom at the time of this excursion both Henry and John Thoreau are reputed to have been in love.

blade of grass was so faithfully reflected; too faithfully indeed for art to imitate, for only Nature may exaggerate herself. The shallowest still water is unfathomable. Wherever the trees and skies are reflected, there is more than Atlantic depth, and no danger of fancy running aground. We notice that it required a separate intention of the eye, a more free and abstracted vision, to see the reflected trees and the sky, than to see the river bottom merely; and so are there manifold visions in the direction of every object, and even the most opaque reflect the heavens from their surface. Some men have their eyes naturally intended to the one and some to the other object.

Two men in a skiff, whom we passed hereabouts, floating buoyantly amid the reflections of the trees, like a feather in mid-air, or a leaf which is wafted gently from its twig to the water without turning over, seemed still in their element, and to have very delicately availed themselves of the natural laws. Their floating there was a beautiful and successful experiment in natural philosophy, and it served to ennoble in our eyes the art of navigation; for as birds fly and fishes swim, so these men sailed. It reminded us how much fairer and nobler all the actions of man might be, and that our life in its whole economy might be as beautiful as the fairest works of art or nature.

The sun lodged on the old gray cliffs, and glanced from every pad; the bulrushes and flags seemed to rejoice in the delicious light and air; the meadows were a-drinking at their leisure; the frogs sat meditating, all sabbath

HENRY
BUGBEE
KANE

thoughts, summing up their week, with one eye out on the golden sun, and one toe upon a reed, eying the wondrous universe in which they act their part; the fishes swam more staid and soberly, as maidens go to church; shoals of golden and silver minnows rose to the surface to behold the heavens, and then sheered off into more sombre aisles; they swept by as if moved by one mind, continually gliding past each other, and yet preserving the form of their battalion unchanged, as if they were still embraced by the transparent membrane which held the spawn; a young band of brethren and sisters trying their new fins; now they wheeled, now shot ahead, and when we drove them to the shore and cut them off, they dexterously tacked and passed underneath the boat. Over the old wooden bridges no traveler crossed, and neither the river nor the fishes avoided to glide between the abutments.

Here was a village not far off behind the woods, Billerica, settled not long ago, and the children still bear the names of the first settlers in this late "howling wilderness;" yet to all intents and purposes it is as old as Fernay or as Mantua, an old gray town where men grow old and sleep already under moss-grown monuments, — outgrow their usefulness. This is ancient Billerica (Villarica?), now in its dotage, named from the English Billericay, and whose Indian name was Shawshine. I never heard that it was young. See, is not nature here gone to decay, farms all run out, meeting-house grown gray and racked with age?

If you would know of its early youth, ask those old gray rocks in the pasture. It has a bell that sounds sometimes as far as Concord woods; I have heard that, — ay, hear it now. No wonder that such a sound startled the dreaming Indian, and frightened his game, when the first bells were swung on trees, and sounded through the forest beyond the plantations of the white man; but to-day I like best the echo amid these cliffs and woods. It is no feeble imitation, but rather its original, or as if some rural Orpheus played over the strain again to show how it should sound.

On the other hand, the road runs up to Carlisle, city of the woods, which, if it is less civil, is the more natural. It does well hold the earth together. It gets laughed at because it is a small town, I know, but nevertheless it is a place where great men may be born any day, for fair winds and foul blow right on over it without distinction. It has a meeting-house and horse-sheds, a tavern and a blacksmith's shop, for centre, and a good deal of wood to cut and cord yet.

And "Bedford, most noble Bedford, I shall not thee forget." History has remembered thee; especially that meek and humble petition of thy old planters, like the wailing of the Lord's own people, "To the gentlemen, the selectmen" of Concord, praying to be erected into a separate parish. We can hardly credit that so plaintive a psalm resounded but little more than a century ago along these Babylonish waters.

"In the extreme difficult seasons of heat and cold," said

they, "we were ready to say of the Sabbath, Behold what a weariness is it." "Gentlemen, if our seeking to draw off proceed from any disaffection to our present Reverend Pastor, or the Christian Society with whom we have taken such sweet counsel together, and walked unto the house of God in company, then hear us not this day; but we greatly desire, if God please, to be eased of our burden on the Sabbath, the travel and fatigue thereof, that the word of God may be nigh to us, near to our houses and in our hearts, that we and our little ones may serve the Lord. We hope that God, who stirred up the spirit of Cyrus to set forward temple work, has stirred us up to ask, and will stir you up to grant, the prayer of our petition; so shall your humble petitioners ever pray, as in duty bound" —

And so the temple work went forward here to a happy conclusion. Yonder in Carlisle the building of the temple was many wearisome years delayed, not that there was wanting of Shittim wood, or the gold of Ophir, but a site therefor convenient to all the worshipers; whether on "Buttrick's Plain," or rather on "Poplar Hill." It was a tedious question.

In this Billerica solid men must have lived, select from year to year; a series of town clerks, at least; and there are old records that you may search. Some spring the white man came, built him a house, and made a clearing here, letting in the sun, dried up a farm, piled up the old gray stones in fences, cut down the pines around his dwelling, planted orchard seeds brought from the old country, and persuaded the civil apple-tree to blossom next to the wild pine and the juniper, shedding its perfume in the wilderness. Their old stocks still remain.

He culled the graceful elm from out the woods and from the river-side, and so refined and smoothed his village plot. He rudely bridged the stream, and drove his team afield into the river meadows, cut the wild grass, and laid bare the homes of beaver, otter, muskrat, and with the whetting of his scythe scared off the deer and bear. He set up a mill, and fields of English grain sprang in the virgin soil. And with his grain he scattered the seeds of the dandelion and the wild trefoil over the meadows, mingling his English flowers with the wild native ones. The bristling burdock, the sweet-scented catnip, and the humble yarrow planted themselves along his woodland road, they, too, seeking "freedom to worship God" in their way. And thus he plants a town.

The white man's mullein soon reigned in Indian cornfields, and sweet-scented English grasses clothed the new soil. Where, then, could the Red Man set his foot? The honey-bee hummed through the Massachusetts woods, and sipped the wild-flowers round the Indian's wigwam, perchance unnoticed, when, with prophetic warning, it stung the Red child's hand, forerunner of that industrious tribe that was to come and pluck the wild-flower of his race up by the root.

The white man comes, pale as the dawn, with a load of thought, with a slumbering intelligence as a fire raked up, knowing well what he knows, not guessing but calculating; strong in community, yielding obedience to authority; of experienced race; of wonderful, wonderful common sense; dull but capable, slow but persevering, severe but just, of little humor but genuine; a laboring man, despising game and sport; building a house that endures, a framed house. He buys the Indian's moccasins and baskets, then buys his hunting-grounds, and at length forgets where he is buried and ploughs up his bones.

And here town records, old, tattered, time-worn, weather-stained chronicles, contain the Indian sachem's mark perchance, an arrow or a beaver, and the few fatal words by which he deeded his hunting-grounds away. He comes with a list of ancient Saxon, Norman, and Celtic names, and strews them up and down this river, — Framingham, Sudbury, Bedford, Carlisle, Billerica, Chelmsford, — and this is New Angle-land, and these are the New West Saxons, whom the Red Men call, not Angle-ish or English, but Yengeese, and so at last they are known for Yankees.

When we were opposite to the middle of Billerica, the fields on either hand had a soft and cultivated English aspect, the village spire being seen over the copses which skirt the river, and sometimes an orchard straggled down to the water-side, though, generally, our course this forenoon was the wildest part of our voyage. It seemed that men led a quiet and very civil life there. The inhabitants were plainly cultivators of the earth, and lived under an organized political government. The school-house stood with a meek aspect, entreating a long truce to war and savage life.

Every one finds by his own experience, as well as in history, that the era in which men cultivate the apple, and the amenities of the garden, is essentially different from that of the hunter and forest life, and neither can displace the other without loss. We have all had our day-dreams, as well as more prophetic nocturnal vision; but as for farming, I am convinced that my genius dates from an older era than the agricultural. I would at least strike my spade into the earth with such careless freedom but accuracy as the woodpecker his bill into a tree. There is in my nature, methinks, a singular yearning toward all wildness. I know of no redeeming qualities in myself but a sincere love for some things, and when I am reproved I fall back on to this ground. What have I to do with ploughs? I cut another furrow than you see. Where the off ox treads, there is it not, it is farther off; where the nigh ox walks, it will not be, it is nigher still. If corn fails, my crop fails not, and what are drought and rain to me?

As we said before, the Concord is a dead stream, but its scenery is the more suggestive to the contemplative voyager, and this day its water was fuller of reflections than our pages even. Just before it reaches the falls in

Billerica, it is contracted, and becomes swifter and shallower, with a yellow pebbly bottom, hardly passable for a canal-boat, leaving the broader and more stagnant portion above like a lake among the hills. All through the Concord, Bedford, and Billerica meadows we had heard no murmur from its stream, except where some tributary runnel tumbled in.

But now at length we heard this staid and primitive river rushing to her fall, like any rill. We here left its channel, just above the Billerica Falls, and entered the canal, which runs, or rather is conducted, six miles through the woods to the Merrimack, at Middlesex; and as we did not care to loiter in this part of our voyage, while one ran along the tow-path drawing the boat by a cord, the other kept it off the shore with a pole, so that we accomplished the whole distance in little more than an hour. This canal, which is the oldest in the country, and has even an antique look beside the more modern railroads, is fed by the Concord, so that we were still

floating on its familiar waters.[1] It is so much water which the river *lets* for the advantage of commerce. There appeared some want of harmony in its scenery, since it was

[1] The Middlesex Canal was the brain child of the Honorable James Sullivan, Attorney General and later Governor of Massachusetts, and of Colonel Loammi Baldwin, an officer of the Revolution. Organized into a public corporation in 1793 the Proprietors commenced digging in the following September. The Canal was completed at a cost in excess of half a million, and Colonel Baldwin opened it at a grand jubilee on the last day of the year 1803. It ran from Charlestown, being there accessible to Boston Harbor, to the Merrimack in Middlesex Village, crossing the Concord, from whence it derived its water, just above Billerica Falls. Being above the level of both the Merrimack and the sea, the system had twenty locks as it passed over eight valleys and rivers suspended in the air by means of aqueducts. Over its twenty-seven-mile course there were scattered fifty-odd bridges. In the course of time the Proprietors, by their extensive financial aid, gained control and completed the construction of the several installations on the Merrimack, so that by the year 1814 a canal boat could be towed, poled, rowed and sailed from Boston to Concord in New Hampshire and return. This trip was made on the average in five days up and four days down. A whole series of landing stages, stores and taverns came into existence at appropriate places for the convenience of shippers and travelers. Several boating companies were organized. Packet boats operated on a regular schedule and there was even a steamboat, the *Merrimack*, specially sponsored by Governor Sullivan. At the peak of its operations in the 1830's, the dividends on the shares of the Proprietors averaged thirty dollars for four years' running. Such was the comprehensive character of this privately financed and maintained inland waterway on which the brothers Thoreau took their week's excursion.

not of equal date with the woods and meadows through which it is led, and we missed the conciliatory influence of time on land and water; but in the lapse of ages, Nature will recover and indemnify herself, and gradually plant fit shrubs and flowers along its borders. Already the kingfisher sat upon a pine over the water, and the bream and pickerel swam below. Thus all works pass directly out of the hands of the architect into the hands of Nature, to be perfected.

It was a retired and pleasant route, without houses or travelers, except some young men who were lounging upon a bridge in Chelmsford, who leaned impudently over the rails to pry into our concerns, but we caught the eye of the most forward, and looked at him till he was visibly discomfited. Not that there was any peculiar efficacy in our look, but rather a sense of shame left in him which disarmed him.

It is a very true and expressive phrase, "He looked daggers at me," for the first pattern and prototype of all daggers must have been a glance of the eye. First, there was the glance of Jove's eye, then his fiery bolt; then, the material gradually hardening, tridents, spears, javelins; and finally, for the convenience of private men, daggers, krisses, and so forth, were invented. It is wonderful how we get about the streets without being wounded by these delicate and glancing weapons, a man can so nimbly whip out his rapier, or without being noticed carry it unsheathed. Yet it is rare that one gets seriously looked at.

As we passed under the last bridge over the canal, just before reaching the Merrimack, the people coming out of church paused to look at us from above, and apparently, so strong is custom, indulged in some heathenish comparisons; but we were the truest observers of this sunny day. According to Hesiod, "The seventh is a holy day, For then Latona brought forth golden-rayed Apollo," and by our reckoning this was the seventh day of the week, and not the first.

I find among the papers of an old Justice of the Peace and Deacon of the town of Concord, this singular memorandum, which is worth preserving as a relic of an ancient custom. After reforming the spelling and grammar, it runs as follows: "Men that traveled with teams on the Sabbath, December 18, 1803, were Jeremiah Richardson and Jonas Parker, both of Shirley. They had teams with rigging such as is used to carry barrels, and they were traveling westward. Richardson was questioned by the Hon. Ephraim Wood, Esq., and he said that Jonas Parker was his fellow-traveler, and he further said that a Mr. Longley was his employer, who promised to bear him out."

We were the men that were gliding northward, this September 1, 1839, with still team, and rigging not the most convenient to carry barrels, unquestioned by any Squire or Church Deacon, and ready to bear ourselves out if need were. In the latter part of the seventeenth century, according to the historian of Dunstable, "Towns were directed to erect '*a cage*' near the meeting-house, and in this all offenders against the sanctity of the Sabbath were confined." Society has relaxed a little from its strictness, one would say, but I presume that there is not less *religion* than formerly. If the *ligature* is found to be loosened in one part, it is only drawn the tighter in another.

By noon we were let down into the Merrimack through the locks at Middlesex, just above Pawtucket Falls, by a serene and liberal-minded man, who came quietly from his book, though his duties, we supposed, did not require him to open the locks on Sundays.[1] With him we had a just and equal encounter of the eyes, as between two honest men.

The movements of the eyes express the perpetual and unconscious courtesy of the parties. It is said that a rogue does not look you in the face, neither does an honest man

---

[1] Here one descended to the level of the Merrimack, or ascended to that of the Canal as the case might be, a height of twenty-five feet in stages through three granite locks, each of which was some eighty feet long. The lock tender at the time of Thoreau's passage was Samuel Page Hadley. There were more locks ahead of them. Above here in the year 1822 there were in operation a total of twenty-five locks, eleven canals and upwards of a dozen dams whereby the boats and rafts by-passed the falls and rapids of the Merrimack. At one stage in a stretch of but nine miles there were six falls. Being locked through was a colorful experience. A contemporary account reads:

"You entered a lock. The gates enclosed you in a damp wooden receptacle, and you seemed to be hopelessly lost to society in the bottom of a mouldy chest. But right ahead of you the water came sizzling and steaming down from above, and you gradually found yourself rising in the world, finally coming up to quite a respectable elevation. Then the gates swung open . . . and you resumed your voyage."

look at you as if he had his reputation to establish. I have seen some who did not know when to turn aside their eyes in meeting yours. A truly confident and magnanimous spirit is wiser than to contend for the mastery in such encounters. Serpents alone conquer by the steadiness of their gaze. My friend looks me in the face and sees me, that is all.

The best relations were at once established between us and this man, and though few words were spoken, he could not conceal a visible interest in us and our excursion. He was a lover of the higher mathematics, as we found, and in the midst of some vast sunny problem, when we overtook him and whispered our conjectures. By this man we were presented with the freedom of the Merrimack. We now felt as if we were fairly launched on the ocean stream of our voyage, and were pleased to find that our boat would float on Merrimack water. We began again busily to put in practice those old arts of rowing, steering, and paddling. It seemed a strange phenomenon to us that the two rivers should mingle their waters so readily, since we had never associated them in our thoughts.

As we glided over the broad bosom of the Merrimack, between Chelmsford and Dracut, at noon, here a quarter of a mile wide, the rattling of our oars was echoed over the water to those villages, and their slight sounds to us. Their harbors lay as smooth and fairy-like as the Lida, or Syracuse, or Rhodes, in our imagination, while, like some strange roving craft, we flitted past what seemed the dwellings of noble home-staying men, seemingly as conspicuous as if on an eminence, or floating upon a tide which came up to those villagers' breasts. At a third of a mile over the water we heard distinctly some children repeating their catechism in a cottage near the shore, while in the broad shallows between, a herd of cows stood lashing their sides, and waging war with the flies.

Two hundred years ago, other catechizing than this was going on here; for here came the Sachem Wannalancet and his people, and sometimes Tahatawan, our Concord Sachem, who afterwards had a church at home, to catch fish at the falls; and here also came John Eliot, with the Bible and Catechism, and Baxter's "Call to the Unconverted," and other tracts, done into the Massachusetts tongue, and taught them Christianity meanwhile.

"This place," says Gookin, referring to Wamesit, "being an ancient and capital seat of Indians, they come to fish; and this good man takes this opportunity to spread the net of the gospel, to fish for their souls." "May 5, 1674," he continues, "according to our usual custom, Mr. Eliot and myself took our journey to Wamesit, or Pawtuckett; and arriving there that evening, Mr. Eliot preached to as many of them as could be got together, out of Matt. xxii. 1–14, the parable of the marriage of the king's son. We met at the wigwam of one called Wannalancet, about two miles from the town, near Pawtuckett falls, and bordering upon Merrimak river. This person, Wannalancet, is the eldest son of old Pasaconaway, the chiefest sachem of Pawtuckett. He is a sober and grave person, and of years, between fifty and sixty. He hath been always loving and friendly to the English."

As yet, however, they had not prevailed on him to embrace the Christian religion.

"But at this time," says Gookin, "May 6, 1674," — "after some deliberation and serious pause, he stood up, and made a speech to this effect: 'I must acknowledge I have, all my days, used to pass in an old canoe, [alluding to his frequent custom to pass in a canoe upon the river,] and now you exhort me to change and leave my old canoe, and embark in a new canoe, to which I have hitherto been unwilling; but now I yield up myself to your advice, and enter into a new canoe, and do engage to pray to God hereafter.' "

One "Mr. Richard Daniel, a gentleman that lived in Billerica," who with other "persons of quality" was present, "desired brother Eliot to tell the sachem from him, that it may be, while he went in his old canoe, he passed in a quiet stream; but the end thereof was death and destruction to soul and body. But now he went into a new canoe, perhaps he would meet with storms and trials, but yet he should be encouraged to persevere, for the end of his voyage would be everlasting rest."

"Since that time, I hear this sachem doth persevere, and is a constant and diligent hearer of God's word, and sanctifieth the Sabbath, though he doth travel to Wamesit meeting every Sabbath, which is above two miles; and though sundry of his people have deserted him, since he subjected to the gospel, yet he continues and persists."[1]

Already, as appears from the records, "At a General Court held at Boston in New England, the 7th of the first month, 1643–44," "Wassamequin, Nashoonon, Kutchamaquin, Massaconomet, and Squaw Sachem, did voluntarily submit themselves" to the English; and among other things did "promise to be willing from time to time to be instructed in the knowledge of God." Being asked "not to do any unnecessary work on the Sabbath day, especially within the gates of Christian towns," they answered, "It is easy to them; they have not much to do on any day, and they can well take their rest on that day."

"So," says Winthrop, in his Journal, "we causing them to understand the articles, and all the ten commandments of God, and they freely assenting to all, they were solemnly received, and then presented the Court with twenty-six fathom more of wampom; and the Court gave each of them a coat of two yards of cloth, and their dinner; and to them and their men, every of them, a cup of sack at

---

[1] *Gookin's Hist. Coll. of the Indians in New England, 1674.* [Thoreau.] This quaint account, written by Daniel Gookin, Gentleman, is stated to have been first printed from the original manuscript in the Collections of the Massachusetts Historical Society, Series 1, Volume 1, 1792, pages 141–224. The quoted passages appear on pages 186–187. [Ed.]

their departure; so they took leave and went away."[1]

What journeyings on foot and on horseback through the wilderness, to preach the gospel to these minks and muskrats! who first, no doubt, listened with their red ears out of a natural hospitality and courtesy, and afterward from curiosity or even interest, till at length there "were praying Indians," and, as the General Court wrote to Cromwell, the "work is brought to this perfection that some of the Indians themselves can pray and prophesy in a comfortable manner."

It was in fact an old battle and hunting ground through which we had been floating, the ancient dwelling-place of a race of hunters and warriors. Their weirs of stone, their arrowheads and hatchets, their pestles, and the mortars in which they pounded Indian corn before the white man had tasted it, lay concealed in the mud of the river bottom. Tradition still points out the spots where they took fish in the greatest numbers, by such arts as they possessed. It is a rapid story the historian will have to put together. Miantonimo, — Winthrop, — Webster. Soon he comes from Montaup to Bunker Hill, from bear-skins, parched corn, bows and arrows, to tiled roofs, wheatfields, guns and swords. Pawtucket and Wamesit, where the Indian resorted in the fishing season, are now Lowell, the city of spindles and Manchester of America, which sends

---

[1] A *Journal of the Transactions and Occurences in the Settlement of Massachusetts and the other New England Colonies from the year 1630–1644*. John Winthrop, Hartford, 1790, page 325.

its cotton cloth round the globe. Even we youthful voyagers had spent a part of our lives in the village of Chelmsford, when the present city, whose bells we heard, was its obscure north district only, and the giant weaver was not yet fairly born. So old are we; so young is it.

We were thus entering the State of New Hampshire on the bosom of the flood formed by the tribute of its innumerable valleys.[1] The river was the only key which could unlock its maze, presenting its hills and valleys, its lakes and streams, in their natural order and position. The Merrimack, or Sturgeon River, is formed by the confluence of the Pemigewasset, which rises near the Notch of the White Mountains, and the Winnipiseogee, which drains the lake of the same name, signifying "The Smile of the Great Spirit." From their junction it runs south seventy-eight miles to Massachusetts, and thence east thirty-five miles to the sea.

I have traced its stream from where it bubbles out of the rocks of the White Mountains above the clouds, to where it is lost amid the salt billows of the ocean on Plum Island beach. At first it comes on murmuring to itself by

[1] The meaning here is prospective for they had only reached the Great Bend of the Merrimack and were still in Massachusetts. The state line lay to the north between the Townships of Tyngsborough in Massachusetts and Hudson and Nashua in New Hampshire. They did not reach this boundary until the next day at noon. See pages 100, 101 and compare page 252 where on Friday week the boundary is mentioned when they passed over it on the return voyage.

the base of stately and retired mountains, through moist primitive woods whose juices it receives, where the bear still drinks it, and the cabins of settlers are far between, and there are few to cross its stream; enjoying in solitude its cascades still unknown to fame; by long ranges of mountains of Sandwich and of Squam, slumbering like tumuli of Titans, with the peaks of Moosehillock, the Haystack, and Kearsarge reflected in its waters; where the maple and the raspberry, those lovers of the hills, flourish amid temperate dews; flowing long and full of meaning, but untranslatable as its name Pemigewasset, by many a pastured Pelion and Ossa, where unnamed muses haunt, tended by Oreads, Dryads, Naiads, and receiving the tribute of many an untasted Hippocrene.

There are earth, air, fire, and water, — very well, this is water, and down it comes, falling all the way, and yet not discouraged by the lowest fall. By the law of its birth never to become stagnant, for it has come out of the clouds, and down the sides of precipices worn in the flood, through beaver-dams broke loose, not splitting but splicing and mending itself, until it found a breathing-place in this low land. There is no danger now that the sun will steal it back to heaven again before it reach the sea, for it has a warrant even to recover its own dews into its bosom again with interest at every eve.

It was already the water of Squam and Newfound Lake and Winnipiseogee, and White Mountain snow dissolved, on which we were floating, and Smith's and Baker's and Mad Rivers, and Nashua and Souhegan and Piscataquoag, and Suncook and Soucook and Contoocook, mingled in incalculable proportions, still fluid, yellowish, restless all, with an ancient, ineradicable inclination to the sea.

So it flows on down by Lowell and Haverhill, at which last place it first suffers a sea change, and a few masts betray the vicinity of the ocean. Between the towns of Amesbury and Newbury it is a broad, commercial river, from a third to half a mile in width, no longer skirted with yellow and crumbling banks, but backed by high green hills and pastures, with frequent white beaches on which the fishermen draw up their nets. I have passed down this portion of the river in a steamboat, and it was a pleasant sight to watch from its deck the fishermen dragging their seines on the distant shore, as in pictures of a foreign strand. At intervals you may meet with a schooner laden with lumber, standing up to Haverhill, or else lying at anchor or aground, waiting for wind or tide; until, at last, you glide under the famous Chain Bridge, and are landed at Newburyport.[1] Thus she who at first was "poore of waters, naked of renowne," having received so many fair tributaries, as was said of the Forth, "Doth grow the greater still, the further downe; Till that abounding both in power and fame, She long doth strive to give the sea her name" — or if not her name, in this case, at least the impulse of her stream. From the steeples of Newburyport you may review this river stretching far up into the country, with many a white sail glancing over it like an inland sea, and behold, as one wrote who was born on its head-waters:

"Down out at its mouth, the dark inky main blending with the blue above. Plum Island, its sand ridges scolloping along the horizon like the sea-serpent, and the distant outline broken by many a tall ship, leaning, *still,* against the sky."

Rising at an equal height with the Connecticut, the Merrimack reaches the sea by a course only half as long, and hence has no leisure to form broad and fertile meadows, like the former, but is hurried along rapids, and down numerous falls, without long delay. The banks are

---

[1] In 1792 a bridge was constructed across the Merrimack from Salisbury to Newbury by the way of Deer Island. That portion of it — a long wooden arch — which ran from this island in the stream to Newbury was later replaced by a chain suspension bridge, from whence the phrase quoted by Thoreau.

generally steep and high, with a narrow intervale reaching back to the hills, which is only rarely or partially overflown at present, and is much valued by the farmers. Between Chelmsford and Concord, in New Hampshire, it varies from twenty to seventy-five rods in width. It is probably wider than it was formerly, in many places, owing to the trees having been cut down, and the consequent wasting away of its banks. The influence of the Pawtucket Dam is felt as far up as Cromwell's Falls, and many think that the banks are being abraded and the river filled up again by this cause. Like all our rivers, it is liable to freshets, and the Pemigewasset has been known to rise twenty-five feet in a few hours. It is navigable for vessels of burden about twenty miles; for canal-boats, by means of locks, as far as Concord in New Hampshire, about seventy-five miles from its mouth; and for smaller boats to Plymouth, one hundred and thirteen miles. A small steamboat once plied between Lowell and Nashua, before the railroad was built, and one now runs from Newburyport to Haverhill.

Unfitted to some extent for the purposes of commerce by the sand-bar at its mouth, see how this river was devoted from the first to the service of manufactures. Issuing from the iron region of Franconia, and flowing through still uncut forests, by inexhaustible ledges of granite, with Squam, and Winnipiseogee, and Newfound, and Massabesic Lakes for its millponds, it falls over a succession of natural dams, where it has been offering its *privileges* in vain for ages, until at last the Yankee race came to *improve* them.

Standing at its mouth, look up its sparkling stream to its source, — a silver cascade which falls all the way from the White Mountains to the sea, — and behold a city on each successive plateau, a busy colony of human beaver around every fall. Not to mention Newburyport and Haverhill, see Lawrence, and Lowell, and Nashua, and Manchester, and Concord, gleaming one above the other. When at length it has escaped from under the last of the factories, it has a level and unmolested passage to the sea, a mere *waste water,* as it were, bearing little with it but its fame; its pleasant course revealed by the morning fog which hangs over it, and the sails of the few small vessels which transact the commerce of Haverhill and Newburyport.

But its real vessels are railroad cars, and its true and main stream, flowing by an iron channel farther south, may be traced by a long line of vapor amid the hills, which no morning wind ever disperses, to where it empties into the sea at Boston. This side is the louder murmur now. Instead of the scream of a fish-hawk scaring the fishes, is heard the whistle of the steam-engine, arousing a country to its progress.

This river too was at length discovered by the white man, "trending up into the land," he knew not how far, possibly an inlet to the South Sea. Its valley, as far as the Winnipiseogee, was first surveyed in 1652. The first settlers of Massachusetts supposed that the Connecticut, in one part of its course, ran northwest, "so near the great lake as the Indians do pass their canoes into it over land." From which lake and the "hideous swamps" about it, as they supposed, came all the beaver that was traded between Virginia and Canada, — and the Potomac was thought to come out of or from very near it. Afterward the Connecticut came so near the course of the Merrimack that, with a little pains, they expected to divert the current of the trade into the latter river, and its profits from their Dutch neighbors into their own pockets.

Unlike the Concord, the Merrimack is not a dead but a living stream, though it has less life within its waters and on its banks. It has a swift current, and, in this part of its course, a clayey bottom, almost no weeds, and comparatively few fishes. We looked down into its yellow water with the more curiosity, who were accustomed to the Nile-like blackness of the former river. Shad and alewives are taken here in their season, but salmon, though at one time more numerous than shad, are now more rare. Bass, also, are taken occasionally; but locks and dams have proved more or less destructive to the fisheries.

The shad make their appearance early in May, at the same time with the blossoms of the pyrus, one of the most conspicuous early flowers, which is for this reason called the shad-blossom. An insect called the shad-fly also appears at the same time, covering the houses and fences. We are told that "their greatest run is when the apple-trees are in full blossom. The old shad return in August; the young, three or four inches long, in September.[1] These are very fond of flies."

A rather picturesque and luxurious mode of fishing was formerly practiced on the Connecticut, at Bellows Falls, where a large rock divides the stream. "On the steep sides of the island rock," says Belknap, "hang several armchairs, fastened to ladders, and secured by a counterpoise, in which fishermen sit to catch salmon and shad with dipping nets."[2] The remains of Indian weirs, made of large stones, are still to be seen in the Winnipiseogee, one of the headwaters of this river.

It cannot but affect our philosophy favorably to be reminded of these shoals of migratory fishes, of salmon, shad, alewives, marsh-bankers, and others, which penetrate up the innumerable rivers of our coast in the spring, even to the interior lakes, their scales gleaming in the sun; and again, of the fry which in still greater numbers wend their way downward to the sea.

---

[1] 1850 is the date usually given when the several dams and the pollution from the mills caused the cessation of fish running up the Merrimack. In his Journal Thoreau corroborates this in part. On April 13, 1853 at Haverhill, he recorded:

"First shad caught at Haverhill today; first alewife the 10th. Fishermen say that no fish can get above the dam at Lawrence. No shad, etc., were caught at Lowell last year."

[2] *The History of New Hampshire,* Jeremy Belknap, A.M. 3 vols., Philadelphia, 1784–1792. Vol. 3 on page 61. This comprehensive and well-written history and description of New Hampshire is, together with Gookin, Hayward's *New England Gazetteer,* Fox's *History of Dunstable,* and Mirick's *History of Haverhill,* the source of Thoreau's historical accounts concerning the settlements in the Merrimack River valley and intervales.

"And is it not pretty sport," wrote Captain John Smith, who was on this coast as early as 1614, "to pull up two-pence, sixpence, and twelvepence, as fast as you can haul and veer a line?" "And what sport doth yield a more pleasing content, and less hurt or charge, than angling with a hook, and crossing the sweet air from isle to isle, over the silent streams of a calm sea." [1]

On the sandy shore, opposite the Glass-house village in Chelmsford, at the Great Bend where we landed to rest us and gather a few wild plums, we discovered the *Campanula rotundifolia*, a new flower to us, the harebell of the poets, which is common to both hemispheres, growing close to the water. Here, in the shady branches of an

[1] *The Generall Historie of Virginia, New England and the Summer Iles etc.*, John Smith, London, 1627, page 219.

apple-tree on the sand, we took our nooning, where there was not a zephyr to disturb the repose of this glorious Sabbath day, and we reflected serenely on the long past and successful labors of Latona.

As we thus rested in the shade, or rowed leisurely along, we had recourse, from time to time, to the Gazetteer, which was our Navigator, and from its bald natural facts extracted the pleasure of poetry. Beaver River comes in a little lower down, draining the meadows of Pelham, Windham, and Londonderry. The Scotch-Irish settlers of the latter town, according to this authority, were the first to introduce the potato into New England, as well as the manufacture of linen cloth.[1]

We thus worked our way up this river, gradually adjusting our thoughts to novelties, beholding from its placid bosom a new nature and new works of men, and, as it were with increasing confidence, finding nature still habitable, genial, and propitious to us; not following any beaten path, but the windings of the river, as ever the nearest way for us. Fortunately we had no business in this country.

---

[1] *The New England Gazetteer,* John Hayward, Concord, N.H. This compendium of local information was Thoreau's *vade mecum,* which he repeatedly quotes or cites hereafter. The notation of a copy appears in an 1840 list of his library made by him and printed in the back of F. B. Sanborn's *The Life of Henry David Thoreau* (1917). The data about the introduction of the potato and the manufacture of linen appears in the edition published in 1839 under the head of Londonderry, N.H.

The Concord had rarely been a river, or *rivus,* but barely *fluvius,* or between *fluvius* and *lacus.* This Merrimack was neither *rivus* nor *fluvius* nor *lacus,* but rather *amnis* here, a gently swelling and stately rolling flood approaching the sea. We could even sympathize with its buoyant tide, going to seek its fortune in the ocean, and, anticipating the time when "being received within the plain of its freer water," it should "beat the shores for banks."

At length we doubled a low shrubby islet, called Rabbit Island, subjected alternately to the sun and to the waves, as desolate as if it lay some leagues within the icy sea, and found ourselves in a narrower part of the river, near the sheds and yards for picking the stone known as the Chelmsford granite, which is quarried in Westford and the neighboring towns. We passed Wicasuck Island, which contains seventy acres or more, on our right, between Chelmsford and Tyngsborough. This was a favorite residence of the Indians.

According to the History of Dunstable, "About 1663, the eldest son of Passaconaway [Chief of the Penacooks] was thrown into jail for a debt of £45, due to John Tinker, by one of his tribe, and which he had promised verbally should be paid. To relieve him from his imprisonment, his brother Wannalancet and others, who owned Wicasuck Island, sold it and paid the debt." It was, however, restored to the Indians by the General Court in 1665.

After the departure of the Indians in 1683, it was granted to Jonathan Tyng in payment for his services to the colony, in maintaining a garrison at his house.[1] Tyng's house stood not far from Wicasuck Falls. Gookin, who, in his Epistle Dedicatory to Robert Boyle, apologizes for presenting his "matter clothed in a wilderness dress," says that on the breaking out of Philip's war in 1675, there were taken up by the Christian Indians and the English in Marlborough, and sent to Cambridge, seven "Indians belonging to Narragansett, Long Island, and Pequod, who had all been at work about seven weeks with one Mr. Jonathan Tyng, of Dunstable, upon Merrimack River; and, hearing of the war, they reckoned with their master, and getting their wages, conveyed themselves away without his privity, and, being afraid, marched secretly through the woods, designing to go to their own country." However, they were released soon after. Such were the hired men in those days.

Tyng was the first permanent settler of Dunstable, which then embraced what is now Tyngsborough and many other towns. In the winter of 1675, in Philip's war, every other settler left the town, but "he," says the historian of Dunstable, "fortified his house; and, although 'obliged to send to Boston for his food,' sat himself down in the midst of his savage enemies, alone, in the wilder-

[1] Wicasuck Island is known today as Tyng's Island according to the *United States Geological Survey* map of Tyngsborough Quadrangle.

ness, to defend his home.[1] Deeming his position an important one for the defense of the frontiers, in February, 1676, he petitioned the Colony for aid," humbly showing, as his petition runs, that, as he lived "in the uppermost house on Merrimack river, lying open to y[e] enemy, yet being so seated that it is, as it were, a watch-house to the neighboring towns," he could render important service to his country if only he had some assistance, "there being," he said, "never an inhabitant left in the town but myself." Wherefore he requests that their "Honors would be pleased to order him *three or four men* to help garrison his said house," which they did. But methinks that such a garrison would be weakened by the addition of a man. Thus he earned the title of first permanent settler.

In 1694 a law was passed "that every settler who deserted a town for fear of the Indians should forfeit all his rights therein." But now, at any rate, as I have frequently observed, a man may desert the fertile frontier territories of truth and justice, which are the State's best lands, for fear of far more insignificant foes, without forfeiting any of his civil rights therein. Nay, townships are granted to deserters, and the General Court, as I am

---

[1] *History of the Old Township of Dunstable,* Charles J. Fox, 1846, Nashua N.H. p. 21. An outpost in the days of the French and Indian Wars, the large township of Dunstable then lay within Massachusetts, its northern bound formed by the course of the Souhegan River, seven miles north of the present location of Nashua, N.H. In 1741 the boundary controversy between the two colonies was settled to the discomfiture of the inhabitants of Dunstable, who saw their township cut in two and its northern portion transferred into New Hampshire.

sometimes inclined to regard it, is but a deserters' camp itself.

As we rowed along near the shore of Wicasuck Island, which was then covered with wood, in order to avoid the current, two men, who looked as if they had just run out of Lowell, where they had been waylaid by the Sabbath, meaning to go to Nashua, and who now found themselves in the strange, natural, uncultivated, and unsettled part of the globe which intervenes, full of walls and barriers, a rough and uncivil place to them, seeing our boat moving so smoothly up the stream, called out from the high bank above our heads to know if we would take them as passengers, as if this were the street they had missed; that they might sit and chat and drive away the time, and so at last find themselves in Nashua. This smooth way they much preferred. But our boat was crowded with necessary furniture, and sunk low in the water, and moreover required to be worked, for even *it* did not progress against the stream without effort; so we were obliged to deny them passage.

As we glided away with even sweeps, while the fates scattered oil in our course, the sun now sinking behind the alders on the distant shore, we could still see them far off over the water, running along the shore and climbing over the rocks and fallen trees like insects, — for they did not know any better than we that they were on an island, — the unsympathizing river ever flowing in an opposite direction; until, having reached the entrance of the island brook, which they had probably crossed upon the locks below, they found a more effectual barrier to their progress. They seemed to be learning much in a little time. They ran about like ants on a burning brand, and once more they tried the river here, and once more there, to see if water still indeed was not to be walked on, as if a new thought inspired them, and by some peculiar disposition of the limbs they could accomplish it. At length sober common sense seemed to have resumed its sway, and they concluded that what they had so long heard must be true, and resolved to ford the shallower stream. When nearly a mile distant we could see them stripping off their clothes and preparing for this experiment; yet it seemed likely that a new dilemma would arise, they were so thoughtlessly throwing away their clothes on the wrong side of the stream, as in the case of the countryman with his corn, his fox, and his goose, which had to be transported one at a time.

Whether they got safely through, or went round by the locks, we never learned. We could not help being struck by the seeming, though innocent indifference of Nature to those men's necessities, while elsewhere she was equally serving others. Like a true benefactress, the secret of her service is unchangeableness. Thus is the busiest merchant, though within sight of his Lowell, put to pilgrim's shifts, and soon comes to staff and scrip and scallop shell.

We, too, who held the middle of the stream, came near

experiencing a pilgrim's fate, being tempted to pursue what seemed a sturgeon or larger fish, for we remembered that this was the Sturgeon River, its dark and monstrous back alternately rising and sinking in midstream. We kept falling behind, but the fish kept his back well out, and did not dive, and seemed to prefer to swim against the stream, so, at any rate, he would not escape us by going out to sea. At length, having got as near as was convenient, and looking out not to get a blow from his tail, now the bow-gunner delivered his charge, while

the stern-man held his ground. But the halibut-skinned monster, in one of these swift-gliding pregnant moments, without ever ceasing his bobbing up and down, saw fit, without a chuckle or other prelude, to proclaim himself a huge imprisoned spar, placed there as a buoy, to warn sailors of sunken rocks. So, each casting some blame upon the other, we withdrew quickly to safer waters.

The Scene-shifter saw fit here to close the drama of this day without regard to any unities which we mortals prize. Whether it might have proved tragedy, or comedy, or tragi-comedy, or pastoral, we cannot tell. This Sunday ended by the going down of the sun, leaving us still on the waves. But they who are on the water enjoy a longer and brighter twilight than they who are on the land, for here the water, as well as the atmosphere, absorbs and reflects the light, and some of the day seems to have sunk down into the waves. The light gradually forsook the deep water, as well as the deeper air, and the gloaming came to the fishes as well as to us, and more dim and gloomy to them, whose day is a perpetual twilight, though sufficiently bright for their weak and watery eyes.

Vespers had already rung in many a dim and watery chapel down below, where the shadows of the weeds were extended in length over the sandy floor. The vespertinal pout had already begun to flit on leathern fin, and the finny gossips withdrew from the fluvial street to creeks and coves, and other private haunts, excepting a few of stronger fin, which anchored in the stream, stemming the tide even in their dreams. Meanwhile, like a dark evening cloud, we were wafted over the cope of their sky, deepening the shadows on their deluged fields.

Having reached a retired part of the river where it spread out to sixty rods in width, we pitched our tent on the east side, in Tyngsborough, just above some patches of the beach plum, which was now nearly ripe, where the sloping bank was a sufficient pillow, and with the bustle of sailors making the land, we transferred such stores as were required from boat to tent, and hung a lantern to the tent-pole, and so our house was ready. With a buffalo spread on the grass, and a blanket for our covering, our bed was soon made. A fire crackled merrily before the entrance, so near that we could tend it without stepping abroad, and when we had supped, we put out the blaze, and closed the door, and with the semblance of domestic comfort, sat up to read the Gazetteer, to learn our latitude and longitude, and write the journal of the voyage, or listened to the wind and the rippling of the river till sleep overtook us.

There we lay under an oak on the bank of the stream, near to some farmer's cornfield, getting sleep, and forgetting where we were; a great blessing, that we are obliged to forget our enterprises every twelve hours. Minks, muskrats, meadow-mice, woodchucks, squirrels, skunks, rabbits, foxes, and weasels, all inhabit near, but keep very close while you are there. The river sucking and eddying away all night down toward the marts and the seaboard, a great wash and freshet, and no small enterprise to reflect on. Instead of the Scythian vastness of the Billerica night, and its wild musical sounds, we were kept awake by the boisterous sport of some Irish laborers on the railroad, wafted to us over the water, still unwearied and unresting on this seventh day, who would not have done with whirling up and down the track with ever-increasing velocity and still reviving shouts, till late in the night.

One sailor was visited in his dreams this night by the Evil Destinies, and all those powers that are hostile to human life, which constrain and oppress the minds of men, and make their path seem difficult and narrow, and beset with dangers, so that the most innocent and worthy enterprises appear insolent and a tempting of fate, and the gods go not with us. But the other happily passed a serene and even ambrosial or immortal night, and his sleep was dreamless, or only the atmosphere of pleasant dreams remained, a happy, natural sleep until the morning; and his cheerful spirit soothed and reassured his brother, for whenever they meet, the Good Genius is sure to prevail.

4. *Monday*

WHEN the first light dawned on the earth, and the birds awoke, and the brave river was heard rippling confidently seaward, and the nimble early rising wind rustled the oak leaves about our tent, all men, having reinforced their bodies and their souls with sleep, and cast aside doubt and fear, were invited to unattempted adventures.

One of us took the boat over to the opposite shore, which was flat and accessible, a quarter of a mile distant, to empty it of water and wash out the clay, while the other kindled a fire and got breakfast ready. At an early hour we were again on our way, rowing through the fog as before, the river already awake, and a million crisped waves come forth to meet the sun when he should show himself. The countrymen, recruited by their day of rest, were already stirring, and had begun to cross the ferry on the business of the week.

This ferry was as busy as a beaver dam, and all the world seemed anxious to get across the Merrimack River at this particular point, waiting to get set over, — children with their two cents done up in paper, jailbirds broke loose and constable with warrant, travelers from distant lands to distant lands, men and women to whom the Merrimack River was a bar.

There stands a gig in the gray morning, in the mist, the impatient traveler pacing the wet shore with whip in hand, and shouting through the fog after the regardless Charon and his retreating ark, as if he might throw that passenger overboard and return forthwith for himself; he will compensate him. He is to break his fast at some unseen place on the opposite side. It may be Ledyard, or the Wandering Jew. Whence, pray, did he come out of the foggy night? and whither through the sunny day will he go? We observe only his transit; important to us, forgotten by him, transiting all day.

There are two of them. May be, they are Virgil and Dante. But when they crossed the Styx, none were seen bound up or down the stream, that I remember. It is only a *transjectus,* a transitory voyage, like life itself, none but the long-lived gods bound up or down the stream. Many of these Monday men are ministers, no doubt, reseeking their parishes with hired horses, with sermons in their valises all read and gutted, the day after never with them. They cross each other's routes all the country over like woof and warp, making a garment of loose texture; vacation now for six days. They stop to pick nuts and berries, and gather apples, by the wayside at their leisure. Good religious men, with the love of men in their hearts, and the means to pay their toll in their pockets. We got over this ferry chain without scraping, rowing athwart the tide of travel, — no toll for us that day.[1]

The fog dispersed, and we rowed leisurely along through Tyngsborough, with a clear sky and a mild atmosphere, leaving the habitations of men behind, and penetrating yet farther into the territory of ancient Dunstable. It was from Dunstable, then a frontier town, that the famous Captain Lovewell, with his company, marched in quest of the Indians on the 18th of April, 1725. He was the son of "an ensign in the army of Oliver Cromwell, who

---

[1] The chain suggests that this ferry may have been of the primitive type still encountered in out-of-the-way localities. Moored to each bank a cable stretches across the stream. On it there runs a heavy block from which lead towing lines. These latter are attached to each end of the scow that serves as a ferry. With a pole this craft is shoved out into the current and then by the use of a sort of windlass amidships, a scoop like a centerboard is set at an angle to the current beneath the bottom. Thereupon the current flowing against and off of this angled keel "sets" her across. The writer of this note has been ferried on such a contraption across the upper St. John River from Maine to New Brunswick. From the location of Thoreau's campground on Sunday night, one infers that this was the Tyngsborough Ferry. Further upstream at this period there were four more ferries in operation: one near Cromwell's Falls; Thornton's Ferry and Reed's Ferry, both of which survive today in the names of small villages on the west bank; and finally there was one near Goff's Falls.

came to this country, and settled at Dunstable, where he died at the great age of one hundred and twenty years." In the shaggy pine forest of Pequawket they met the "rebel Indians," and prevailed, after a bloody fight, and a remnant returned home to enjoy the fame of their victory. A township called Lovewell's Town, but now, for some reason, or perhaps without reason, Pembroke, was granted them by the State.

Our brave forefathers have exterminated all the Indians, and their degenerate children no longer dwell in garrisoned houses nor hear any war-whoop in their path. We have need to be as sturdy pioneers still as Miles Standish, or Church, or Lovewell. We are to follow on another trail, it is true, but one as convenient for ambushes. What if the Indians are exterminated, are not savages as grim prowling about the clearings to-day?

But they did not all "safe arrive in Dunstable the thirteenth," or the fifteenth, or the thirtieth "day of May." Eleazer Davis and Josiah Jones, both of Concord, for our native town had seven men in this fight, Lieutenant Farwell, of Dunstable, and Jonathan Frye, of Andover, who were all wounded, were left behind, creeping toward the settlements. "After traveling several miles, Frye was left and lost," though a more recent poet has assigned him company in his last hours.

Farwell held out eleven days. "A tradition says," as we learn from the History of Concord, "that arriving at a pond with Lieut. Farwell, Davis pulled off one of his moccasins, cut it in strings, on which he fastened a hook, caught some fish, fried and ate them. They refreshed him, but were injurious to Farwell, who died soon after." Davis had a ball lodged in his body, and his right hand shot off; but on the whole he seems to have been less damaged than his companions. He came into Berwick after being out fourteen days. Jones also had a ball lodged in his body, but he likewise got into Saco after fourteen days, though not in the best condition imaginable. "He had subsisted," says an old journal,[1] "on the spontaneous vegetables of the forest; and cranberries which he had eaten came out of wounds he had received in his body." This was also the case with Davis. The last two reached home at length, safe if not sound, and lived many years in a crippled state to enjoy their pension.

But alas! of the crippled Indians, and their adventures in the woods, — how many balls lodged with them, how fared their cranberries, what Berwick or Saco they got into, and finally what pension or township was granted them, there is no journal to tell. It is stated in the History of Dunstable that just before his last march, Lovewell was warned to beware of the ambuscades of the enemy, but "he replied, 'that he did not care for them,' and bending down a small elm beside which he was standing into

[1] *A History of the Town of Concord,* Lemuel Shattuck, Concord, 1835, page 68. The old journal is cited by Shattuck as Smith's Journal.

a bow, declared 'that he would treat the Indians in the same way.' This elm is still standing [in Nashua], a venerable and magnificent tree."

Meanwhile, having passed the Horseshoe Intervale, in Tyngsborough, where the river makes a sudden bend to the northwest, — for our reflections have anticipated our progress somewhat, — we were advancing farther into the country and into the day, which last proved almost as golden as the preceding, though the slight bustle and activity of the Monday seemed to penetrate even to this scenery. Now and then we had to muster all our energy to get round a point, where the river broke rippling over rocks, and the maples trailed their branches in the stream, but there was generally a backwater or eddy on the side, of which we took advantage. The river was here about forty rods wide and fifteen feet deep.

Occasionally one ran along the shore, examining the country, and visiting the nearest farm-houses, while the other followed the windings of the stream alone, to meet his companion at some distant point, and hear the report of his adventures; how the farmer praised the coolness of his well, and his wife offered the stranger a draught of milk, or the children quarreled for the only transparency in the window that they might get sight of the man at the well. For though the country seemed so new, and no house was observed by us, shut in between the banks that sunny day, we did not have to travel far to find where men inhabited, like wild bees, and had sunk wells in the loose sand and loam of the Merrimack.

There dwelt the subject of the Hebrew scriptures, and the Esprit des Lois, where a thin, vaporous smoke curled up through the noon. All this is told of mankind, of the inhabitants of the Upper Nile, and the Sunderbunds, and Timbuctoo, and the Orinoko, was experience here. Every race and class of men was represented. According to Belknap, the historian of New Hampshire, who wrote sixty years ago, here too, perchance, dwelt "new lights" and free-thinking men, even then.

"The people in general throughout the State," it is written, "are professors of the Christian religion in some form or other. There is, however, a sort of *wise men* who pretend to reject it; but they have not yet been able to substitute a better in its place."

The other voyageur, perhaps, would in the mean while have seen a brown hawk, or a woodchuck, or a musquash

creeping under the alders. We occasionally rested in the shade of a maple or a willow, and drew forth a melon for our refreshment, while we contemplated at our leisure the lapse of the river and of human life; and as that current, with its floating twigs and leaves, so did all things pass in review before us, while far away in cities and marts on this very stream, the old routine was proceeding still.

There is, indeed, a tide in the affairs of men, as the poet says, and yet as things flow they circulate, and the ebb always balances the flow. All streams are but tributary to the ocean, which itself does not stream, and the shores are unchanged, but in longer periods than man can measure. Go where we will, we discover infinite change in particulars only, not in generals. When I go into a museum and see the mummies wrapped in their linen bandages, I see that the lives of men began to need reform as long ago as when they walked the earth. I come out into the streets, and meet men who declare that the time is near at head for the redemption of the race. But as men lived in Thebes, so do they live in Dunstable today.[1]

While engaged in these reflections, thinking ourselves the only navigators of these waters, suddenly a canal-boat,

---

[1] Here occurs a digression in the form of a dissertation upon Hindu philosophy. The frame of *A Week on the Concord and Merrimack Rivers* is slight — a chronological account of the excursion compressing the two weeks into one and confining it in chief to the river trip. Then, as every critic from James Russell Lowell to F. O. Matthiessen has

with its sail set, glided round a point before us, like some huge river beast, and changed the scene in an instant; and then another and another glided into sight, and we found ourselves in the current of commerce once more. So we threw our rinds in the water for the fishes to nibble, and added our breath to the life of living men. Little did we think, in the distant garden in which we had planted the seed and reared this fruit, where it would be eaten. Our melons lay at home on the sandy bottom of the Merrimack, and our potatoes in the sun and water at the bottom of the boat looked like a fruit of the country.

Soon, however, we were delivered from this fleet of junks, and possessed the river in solitude, once more rowing steadily upward through the noon, between the territories of Nashua on the one hand, and Hudson, once Nottingham, on the other. From time to time we scared up a kingfisher or a summer duck, the former flying rather by vigorous impulses than by steady and patient steering

---

noted, Thoreau at some later stage interleaved and wove into his narrative a lecture on this and an essay on that — Chaucer, Friendship, Goethe, Anacreon, Hindoo Philosophy — "The casual pouring in," says Matthiessen, "of miscellaneous poems and essays that Thoreau had previously printed in *The Dial*," described by Henry Seidel Canby as "these stored-up manuscripts . . . dropped like coins into an open purse." "We come upon them," wrote Lowell "like snags . . . " that . . . "mar our Merrimacking dreadfully. We were bid to a river-party — not to be preached at." The present volume is not another edition of the *Week*. Properly described as excerpts from the *Week*, rather does it comprise a careful selection of those passages which, when they are allowed to come into juxtaposition, give to the reader without interruption a connected account of this first excursion of Henry David Thoreau. This process has been followed with scrupulous regard for the integrity of his text.

with that short rudder of his, sounding his rattle along the fluvial street.

Erelong another scow hove in sight, creeping down the river; and hailing it, we attached ourselves to its side, and floated back in company, chatting with the boatmen, and obtaining a draught of cooler water from their jug. They appeared to be green hands from far among the hills, who had taken this means to get to the seaboard, and see the world; and would possibly visit the Falkland Isles, and the China seas, before they again saw the waters of the Merrimack, or, perchance, they would not return this way forever. They had already embarked the private interests of the landsman in the larger venture of the race, and were ready to mess with mankind, reserving only the till of a chest to themselves. But they too were soon lost behind a point, and we went croaking on our way alone. What grievance has its root among the New Hampshire hills? we asked; what is wanting to human life here, that these men should make such haste to the antipodes? We prayed that their bright anticipations might not be rudely disappointed.

We passed a small desert here on the east bank, between Tyngsborough and Hudson, which was interesting and even refreshing to our eyes in the midst of the almost universal greenness. This sand was indeed somewhat impressive and beautiful to us. A very old inhabitant, who was at work in a field on the Nashua side, told us that he remembered when corn and grain grew there, and it was

HENRY
BUGBEE
KANE

a cultivated field. But at length the fishermen, for this was a fishing-place, pulled up the bushes on the shore, for greater convenience in hauling their seines, and when the bank was thus broken, the wind began to blow up the sand from the shore, until at length it had covered about fifteen acres several feet deep.

We saw near the river, where the sand was blown off down to some ancient surface, the foundation of an Indian wigwam exposed, a perfect circle of burnt stones, four or five feet in diameter, mingled with fine charcoal, and the bones of small animals which had been preserved in the sand. The surrounding sand was sprinkled with other burnt stones on which their fires had been built, as well as with flakes of arrow-head stone, and we found one perfect arrow-head. In one place we noticed where an Indian had sat to manufacture arrow-heads out of quartz, and the sand was sprinkled with a quart of small glass-like chips about as big as a fourpence, which he had broken off in his work. Here, then, the Indians must have fished before the whites arrived. There was another similar sandy tract about half a mile above this.

Still the noon prevailed, and we turned the prow aside to bathe, and recline ourselves under some buttonwoods, by a ledge of rocks, in a retired pasture sloping to the water's edge, and skirted with pines and hazels, in the town of Hudson. Still had India, and that old noontide philosophy, the better part of our thoughts.

Thus did one voyageur waking dream, while his companion slumbered on the bank.[1] Suddenly a boatman's horn was heard echoing from shore to shore, to give notice of his approach to the farmer's wife with whom he was to take his dinner, though in that place only muskrats and kingfishers seemed to hear. The current of our reflections and our slumbers being thus disturbed, we weighed anchor once more.

As we proceeded on our way in the afternoon, the western bank became lower, or receded farther from the channel in some places, leaving a few trees only to fringe the water's edge; while the eastern rose abruptly here and there into wooded hills fifty or sixty feet high. The bass (*Tilia Americana*), also called the lime or linden, which was a new tree to us, overhung the water with its broad and rounded leaf, interspersed with clusters of small hard berries now nearly ripe, and made an agreeable shade for us sailors. The inner bark of this genus is the bast, the material of the fisherman's matting, and the ropes and peasant's shoes of which the Russians make so much use, and also of nets and a coarse cloth in some places. According to poets, this was once Philyra, one of the Oceanides.

The ancients are said to have used its bark for the roofs of cottages, for baskets, and for a kind of paper called Philyra. They also made bucklers of its wood, "on account

[1] This sentence refers to a further exploration of Indian philosophy.

of its flexibility, lightness, and resiliency." It was once much used for carving, and is still in demand for sounding-boards of piano-fortes and panels of carriages, and for various uses for which toughness and flexibility are required. Baskets and cradles are made of the twigs. Its sap affords sugar, and the honey made from its flowers is said to be preferred to any other. Its leaves are in some countries given to cattle, a kind of chocolate has been made of its fruit, a medicine has been prepared from an infusion of its flowers, and finally, the charcoal made of its wood is greatly valued for gunpowder.

The sight of this tree reminded us that we had reached a strange land to us. As we sailed under this canopy of leaves, we saw the sky through its chinks, and, as it were, the meaning and idea of the tree stamped in a thousand hieroglyphics on the heavens. The universe is so aptly fitted to our organization that the eye wanders and reposes at the same time. On every side there is something to soothe and refresh this sense. Look up at the tree-tops, and see how finely Nature finishes off her work there. See how the pines spire without end higher and higher, and make a graceful fringe to the earth. And who shall count the finer cobwebs that soar and float away from their utmost tops, and the myriad insects that dodge between them. Leaves are of more various forms than the alphabets of all languages put together; of the oaks alone there are hardly two alike, and each expresses its own character.

In all her products, Nature only develops her simplest germs. One would say that it was no great stretch of invention to create birds. The hawk, which now takes his flight over the top of the wood, was at first, perchance, only a leaf which fluttered in its aisles. From rustling leaves she came in the course of ages to the loftier flight and clear carol of the bird.

Salmon Brook comes in from the west under the railroad, a mile and a half below the village of Nashua. We rowed up far enough into the meadows which border it to learn its piscatorial history from a haymaker on its banks. He told us that the silver eel was formerly abundant here, and pointed to some sunken creels at its mouth. This man's memory and imagination were fertile in fishermen's tales of floating isles in bottomless ponds, and of lakes mysteriously stocked with fishes, and would have kept us till nightfall to listen, but we could not afford to loiter in this roadstead, and so stood out to our sea again. Though we never trod in those meadows, but only touched their margin with our hands, we still retain a pleasant memory of them.

Salmon Brook, whose name is said to be a translation from the Indian, was a favorite haunt of the aborigines. Here, too, the first white settlers of Nashua planted, and some dents in the earth where their houses stood and the wrecks of ancient apple-trees are still visible. About one mile up this stream stood the house of old John Lovewell, who was an ensign in the army of Oliver Cromwell, and the father of "famous Captain Lovewell." He settled here before 1690, and died about 1754, at the age of one hundred and twenty years. He is thought to have been engaged in the famous Narragansett swamp fight, which took place in 1675, before he came here. The Indians are said to have spared him in succeeding wars on account of his kindness to them. Even in 1700 he was so old and gray-headed that his scalp was worth nothing, since the French governor offered no bounty for such.

I have stood in the dent of his cellar on the bank of the brook, and talked there with one whose grandfather had, whose father might have, talked with Lovewell. Here also he had a mill in his old age, and kept a small store. He was remembered by some who were recently living, as a hale old man who drove the boys out of his orchard with his cane. Consider the triumphs of the mortal man, and what poor trophies it would have to show, to wit: He cobbled shoes without glasses at a hundred, and cut a handsome swath at a hundred and five! Lovewell's house is said to have been the first which Mrs. Dustan reached on her escape from the Indians. Here, probably, the hero of Pequawket was born and bred.

Close by may be seen the cellar and the gravestone of Joseph Hassell, who, as is elsewhere recorded, with his wife Anna, and son Benjamin, and Mary Marks, "were slain by our Indian enemies on September 2, [1691,] in the evening." As Gookin observed on a previous occasion, "The Indian rod upon the English backs had not yet done

God's errand." Salmon Brook near its mouth is still a solitary stream, meandering through woods and meadows, while the then uninhabited mouth of the Nashua now resounds with the din of a manufacturing town.

A stream from Otternic Pond in Hudson comes in just above Salmon Brook, on the opposite side. There was a good view of Uncannunuc, the most conspicuous mountain in these parts, from the bank here, seen rising over the west end of the bridge above. We soon after passed the village of Nashua, on the river of the same name,

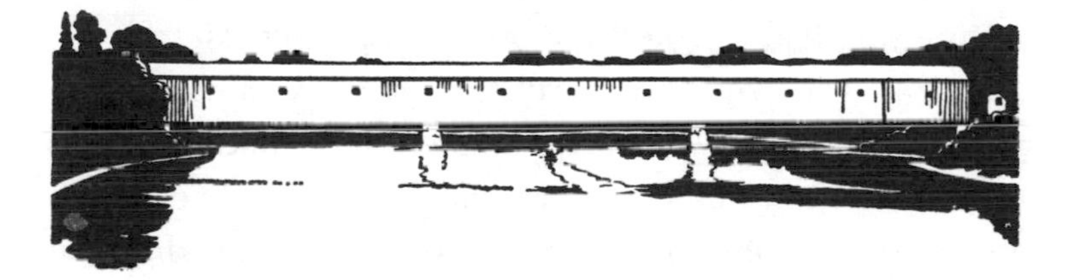

where there is a covered bridge over the Merrimack. The Nashua, which is one of the largest tributaries, flows from Wachusett Mountain, through Lancaster, Groton, and other towns, where it has formed well-known elm-shaded meadows, but near its mouth it is obstructed by falls and factories, and did not tempt us to explore it.

Far away from here, in Lancaster, with another companion, I have crossed the broad valley of the Nashua, over which we had so long looked westward from the Concord hills without seeing it to the blue mountains in the horizon. So many streams, so many meadows and woods and quiet dwellings of men had lain concealed between us and those Delectable Mountains; — from yonder hill on the road to Tyngsborough you may get a good view of them. There where it seemed uninterrupted forest to our youthful eyes, between two neighboring pines in the horizon, lay the valley of the Nashua, and this very stream was even then winding at its bottom, and then, as now, it was here silently mingling its waters with the Merrimack.

The clouds which floated over its meadows and were born there, seen far in the west, gilded by the rays of the setting sun, had adorned a thousand evening skies for us. But as it were, by a turf wall this valley was concealed, and in our journey to those hills it was first gradually revealed to us. Summer and winter our eyes had rested on the dim outline of the mountains, to which distance and indistinctness lent a grandeur not their own, so that they served to interpret all the allusions of poets and travelers.

At length, like Rasselas and other inhabitants of happy valleys, we had resolved to scale the blue wall which bounded the western horizon, though not without misgivings that thereafter no visible fairy-land would exist for us. But it would be long to tell of our adventures, and we have no time this afternoon, transporting ourselves in imagination up this hazy Nashua valley, to go over again that pilgrimage. We have since made many similar excursions to the principal mountains of New England and

New York, and even far in the wilderness, and have passed a night on the summit of many of them. And now, when we look again westward from our native hills, Wachusett and Monadnock have retreated once more among the blue and fabulous mountains in the horizon, though our eyes rest on the very rocks on both of them, where we have pitched our tent for a night, and boiled our hasty-pudding amid the clouds.

As late as 1724 there was no house on the north side of the Nashua, but only scattered wigwams and grisly forests between this frontier and Canada. In September of that year, two men who were engaged in making turpentine on that side, — for such were the first enterprises in the wilderness, — were taken captive and carried to Canada by a party of thirty Indians. Ten of the inhabitants of Dunstable, going to look for them, found the hoops of their barrel cut, and the turpentine spread on the ground.

I have been told by an inhabitant of Tyngsborough, who had the story from his ancestors, that one of these captives, when the Indians were about to upset his barrel of turpentine, seized a pine knot and, flourishing it, swore so resolutely that he would kill the first who touched it, that they refrained, and when at length he returned from Canada he found it still standing. Perhaps there was more than one barrel. However this may have been, the scouts knew by marks on the trees, made with coal mixed with grease, that the men were not killed, but taken prisoners.

One of the company, named Farwell, perceiving that the turpentine had not done spreading, concluded that the Indians had been gone but a short time, and they accordingly went in instant pursuit. Contrary to the advice of Farwell, following directly on their trail up the Merrimack, they fell into an ambuscade near Thornton's Ferry, in the present town of Merrimack, and nine were killed, only one, Farwell, escaping after a vigorous pursuit. The men of Dunstable went out and picked up their bodies, and carried them all down to Dunstable and buried them.

You may read in the churchyard at Dunstable, under the "Memento Mori," and the name of one of them, how they "departed this life," and: "This man with seven more that lies in this grave was slew all in a day by the Indians." The stones of some others of the company stand around the common grave with their separate inscriptions. Eight were buried here, but nine were killed, according to the best authorities.

It is related in the History of Dunstable, that on the return of Farwell the Indians were engaged by a fresh party, which they compelled to retreat, and pursued as far as the Nashua, where they fought across the stream at its mouth. After the departure of the Indians, the figure of an Indian's head was found carved by them on a large tree by the shore, which circumstance has given its name to this part of the village of Nashville, — the "Indian Head."

"It was observed by some judicious," says Gookin, referring to Philip's war, "that at the beginning of the war the English soldiers made a nothing of the Indians, and many spake words to this effect, that one Englishman was sufficient to chase ten Indians; many reckoned it was no other but *Veni, vidi, vici.*" But we may conclude that the judicious would by this time have made a different observation.

Farwell appears to have been the only one who had studied his profession, and understood the business of hunting Indians. He lived to fight another day, for the next year he was Lovewell's lieutenant at Pequawket, but that time, as we have related, he left his bones in the wilderness. His name still reminds us of twilight days and forest scouts on Indian trails, with an uneasy scalp; — an indispensable hero to New England.

These battles sound incredible to us. I think that posterity will doubt if such things ever were; if our bold ancestors who settled this land were not struggling rather with the forest shadows, and not with a copper-colored race of men. They were vapors, fever and ague of the unsettled woods. Now, only a few arrow-heads are turned up by the plough. In the Pelasgic, the Etruscan, or the British story, there is nothing so shadowy and unreal.

It is a wild and antiquated looking graveyard, overgrown with bushes, on the high-road, about a quarter of a mile from and overlooking the Merrimack, with a deserted mill-stream bounding it on one side, where lie the earthly remains of the ancient inhabitants of Dunstable. We passed it three or four miles below here. You may read there the names of Lovewell, Farwell, and many

others whose families were distinguished in Indian warfare. We noticed there two large masses of granite more than a foot thick and rudely squared, lying flat on the ground over the remains of the first pastor and his wife.

It is remarkable that the dead lie everywhere under stones, "Strata jacent passim *suo* quæque sub *lapide*" — *corpora,* we might say, if the measure allowed. When the stone is a slight one, it does not oppress the spirits of the traveler to meditate by it; but these did seem a little heathenish to us; and so are all large monuments over men's bodies, from the pyramids down. A monument should at least be "star-y-pointing," to indicate whither the spirit has gone, and not prostrate, like the body it has deserted. There have been some nations who could do nothing but construct tombs, and these are the only traces which they have left. They are the heathen. But why these stones, so upright and emphatic, like exclamation-points? What was there so remarkable that lived? Why should the monument be so much more enduring than the fame which it is designed to perpetuate, — a stone to a bone?

"Here lies," — "Here lies;" — why do they not sometimes write, There rises? Is it a monument to the body only that is intended? "Having reached the term of his *natural* life;" — would it not be truer to say, Having reached the term of his *unnatural* life? The rarest quality in an epitaph is truth. If any character is given, it should be severely true [illegible] and not the partial testimony of friends. Friends and contemporaries should supply only the name and date, and leave it to posterity to write the epitaph. Fame itself is but an epitaph; as late, as false, as true. But they only are the true epitaphs which Old Mortality retouches.

A man might well pray that he may not taboo or curse any portion of nature by being buried in it. For the most part, the best man's spirit makes a fearful sprite to haunt his grave, and it is therefore much to the credit of Little John, the famous follower of Robin Hood, and reflecting favorably on his character, that his grave was "long celebrous for the yielding of excellent whetstones." I confess that I have but little love for such collections as they have at the Catacombs, Père la Chaise, Mount Auburn, and even this Dunstable graveyard. At any rate, nothing but great antiquity can make graveyards interesting to me. I have no friends there. It may be that I am not competent to write the poetry of the grave. The farmer who has skimmed his farm might perchance leave his body to Nature to be ploughed in, and in some measure restore its fertility. We should not retard but forward her economies.[1]

---

[1] This ancient graveyard, with Spit Brook running past its northerly bound, slopes toward road and river presenting today the precise scene which Thoreau here describes a century ago. Two decades later he would revisit this spot. On July 2, 1858, his Journal records: "Start for White Mountains in a private carriage with Edward Hoar." Hoar had been his companion on his last excursion in the Maine woods the summer before. There follow the ensuing passages:

"Spent the noon close by the old Dunstable graveyard, by a small stream north of it. Red lilies were abundantly in bloom in the burying-ground and by the river. Mr. Weld's monument is a large, thick, naturally flat rock, lying flat over the grave. Noticed the monument of Josiah Willard, Esq., "Captain of Fort Dummer." Died 1750, aged 58. Walked to and along the river and bathed in it.

"What a relief and expansion of my thoughts when I come out from that inland position by the graveyard to this broad river's shore. This vista was incredible there. Suddenly I see a broad reach of blue beneath, with its curves and headlands, liberating me from the more terrene earth. What a difference it makes whether I spend my four hours nooning between the hills by yonder roadside, or on the brink of this fair river, within a quarter of a mile of that! Here the earth is fluid to my thought, the sky is reflected from beneath, and around yonder cape is the highway to other continents. This current allies me to all the world. Be careful to sit in an elevating and inspiring place. There my thoughts were confined and trivial, and I hid myself from the gaze of travelers. Here they are expanded and elevated, and I am charmed by the beautiful river reach. It is equal to a different season and country and creates a different mood.

"As you travel northward from Concord, probably the reaches of the Merrimack River, looking up or down them from the bank, will be the first inspiring sight. There is something in the scenery of a broad river equivalent to culture and civilization. Its channel conducts our thoughts as well as bodies to classic and famous ports, and allies us to all that is

Soon the village of Nashua was out of sight, and the woods were gained again, and we rowed slowly on before sunset, looking for a solitary place in which to spend the night. A few evening clouds began to be reflected in the water, and the surface was dimpled only here and there by a muskrat crossing the stream. We camped at length near Penichook Brook, on the confines of what is now Nashville, by a deep ravine, under the skirts of a pine wood, where the dead pine-leaves were our carpet, and their tawny boughs stretched overhead. But fire and smoke soon tamed the scene; the rocks consented to be our walls, and the pines our roof. A woodside was already the fittest locality for us.

The wilderness is near as well as dear to every man. Even the oldest villages are indebted to the border of wild wood which surrounds them, more than to the gardens of men. There is something indescribably inspiriting and beautiful in the aspect of the forest skirting and occasionally jutting into the midst of new towns, which, like the sand-heaps of fresh fox-burrows, have sprung up in their midst. The very uprightness of the pines and maples asserts the ancient rectitude and vigor of nature. Our

---

fair and great. I like to remember that at the end of half a day's walk I can stand on the bank of the Merrimack. It is just wide enough to interrupt the land and lead my eyes and thoughts down its channel to the sea. A river is superior to a lake in its liberating influence. It has motion and indefinite length. A river touching the back of a town is like a wing, it may be unused as yet, but ready to waft it over the world. With its rapid current it is a slightly fluttering wing. River towns are winged towns."

lives need the relief of such a background, where the pine flourishes and the jay still screams.

We had found a safe harbor for our boat, and as the sun was setting carried up our furniture, and soon arranged our house upon the bank, and while the kettle steamed at the tent door, we chatted of distant friends and of the sights which we were to behold, and wondered which way the towns lay from us. Our cocoa was soon boiled, and supper set upon our chest, and we lengthened out this meal, like old voyageurs, with our talk. Meanwhile we spread the map on the ground, and read in the Gazetteer when the first settlers came here and got a township granted.

Then, when supper was done and we had written the journal of our voyage, we wrapped our buffaloes about us and lay down with our heads pillowed on our arms, listening awhile to the distant baying of a dog, or the murmurs of the river, or to the wind, which had not gone to rest, or half awake and half asleep, dreaming of a star which glimmered through our cotton roof. Perhaps at midnight one was awakened by a cricket shrilly singing on his shoulder, or by a hunting spider in his eye, and was lulled asleep again by some streamlet purling its way along at the bottom of a wooded and rocky ravine in our neighborhood. It was pleasant to lie with our heads so low in the grass, and hear what a tinkling ever-busy laboratory it was. A thousand little artisans beat on their anvils all night long.

Far in the night, as we were falling asleep on the bank

of the Merrimack, we heard some tyro beating a drum incessantly, in preparation for a country muster, as we learned, and we thought of the line, — "When the drum beat at dead of night." We could have assured him that his beat would be answered, and the forces be mustered. Fear not, thou drummer of the night, we too will be there. And still he drummed on in the silence and the dark. This stray sound from a far-off sphere came to our ears from time to time, far, sweet, and significant, and we listened with such an unprejudiced sense as if for the first time we heard at all. No doubt he was an insignificant drummer enough, but his music afforded us a prime and leisure hour, and we felt that we were in season wholly. These simple sounds related us to the stars.

Ay, there was a logic in them so convincing that the combined sense of mankind could never make me doubt their conclusions. I stop my habitual thinking, as if the plough had suddenly run deeper in its furrow through the crust of the world. How can I go on, who have just stepped over such a bottomless skylight in the bog of my life? Suddenly old Time winked at me, — Ah, you know me, you rogue, — and news had come that IT was well. That ancient universe is in such capital health, I think undoubtedly it will never die. Heal yourselves, doctors; by God I live.

Traveling on foot very early one morning due east from here about twenty miles, from Caleb Harriman's tavern in Hampstead toward Haverhill, when I reached the railroad in Plaistow, I heard at some distance a faint music in the air like an Æolian harp, which I immediately suspected to proceed from the cord of the telegraph vibrating in the just awakening morning wind, and applying my ear to one of the posts I was convinced that it was so. It was the telegraph harp singing its message through the country, its message sent not by men, but by gods.

Perchance, like the statue of Memnon, it resounds only in the morning, when the first rays of the sun fall on it. It was like the first lyre or shell heard on the sea-shore, — that vibrating cord high in the air over the shores of earth. So have all things their higher and their lower uses. I heard a fairer news than the journals ever print. It told of things worthy to hear, and worthy of the electric fluid to carry the news of, not of the price of cotton and flour, but it hinted at the price of the world itself and of things which are priceless, of absolute truth and beauty.[1]

---

[1] What he called the "telegraph harp" never failed to fascinate Thoreau. On March 12, 1852, he recorded: "The telegraph harp has spoken to me more distinctly and effectually than any man ever did," and in January of the same year one finds this passage:

"A spirit sweeps the string of the telegraph harp, and strains of music are drawn out endlessly like the wire itself. We have no need to refer music and poetry to Greece for an origin now? What becomes of the story of a tortoise-shell on the seashore now? The world is young, and music is its infant voice. I do not despair of such a world where you have only to stretch an ordinary wire from tree to tree to hear such strains drawn from it by New England breezes as make Greece and all antiquity seem poor in melody. Why was it made that man should be thrilled to his inmost being by the vibrating of a wire? Are not inspiration and ecstasy a more rapid vibration of the nerves swept by the inrushing excited spirit, whether zephyral or boreal in its character."

Still the drum rolled on, and stirred our blood to fresh extravagance that night. The clarion sound and clang of corselet and buckler were heard from many a hamlet of the soul, and many a knight was arming for the fight behind the encamped stars.

There was a high wind this night, which we afterwards learned had been still more violent elsewhere, and had done much injury to the cornfields far and near; but we only heard it sigh from time to time, as if it had no license to shake the foundations of our tent; the pines murmured, the water rippled, and the tent rocked a little, but we only laid our ears closer to the ground, while the blast swept on to alarm other men, and long before sunrise we were ready to pursue our voyage as usual.

5. *Tuesday*

LONG before daylight we ranged abroad, hatchet in hand, in search of fuel, and made the yet slumbering and dreaming wood resound with our blows. Then with our fire we burned up a portion of the loitering night, while the kettle sang its homely strain to the morning star. We tramped about the shore, waked all the muskrats, and scared up the bittern and birds that were asleep upon their roosts; we hauled up and upset our boat, and washed it and rinsed out the clay, talking aloud as if it were broad day, until at length, by three o'clock, we had completed our preparations and were ready to pursue our voyage as usual; so, shaking the clay from our feet, we pushed into the fog. Though we were enveloped in mist as usual, we trusted that there was a bright day behind it.

Belknap, the historian of this State, says that, "In the neighborhood of fresh rivers and ponds, a whitish fog in the morning lying over the water is a sure indication of fair weather for that day; and when no fog is seen, rain is expected before night." That which seemed to us to invest the world was only a narrow and shallow wreath of vapor stretched over the channel of the Merrimack from the seaboard to the mountains. More extensive fogs, however, have their own limits. I once saw the day break from the top of Saddle-back Mountain in Massachusetts, above the clouds.[1] As we cannot distinguish objects through this dense fog, let me tell this story more at length.

I had come over the hills on foot and alone in serene summer days, plucking the raspberries by the wayside, and occasionally buying a loaf of bread at a farmer's house, with a knapsack on my back which held a few traveler's books and a change of clothing, and a staff in my hand. I had that morning looked down from the Hoosack Mountain, where the road crosses it, on the village of North Adams in the valley three miles away under my feet, showing how uneven the earth may sometimes be, and making it seem an accident that it should ever be

[1] From Thoreau's description this is identified as Mount Greylock (3535 alt.) the highest point of land in the Berkshires and in Massachusetts. The Appalachian Trail passes near its summit and it is today in winter a mecca for the skiing fraternity.

level and convenient for the feet of man. Putting a little rice and sugar and a tin cup into my knapsack at this village, I began in the afternoon to ascend the mountain, whose summit is three thousand six hundred feet above the level of the sea, and was seven or eight miles distant by the path.

My route lay up a long and spacious valley called the Bellows, because the winds rush up or down it with violence in storms, sloping up to the very clouds between the principal range and a lower mountain. There were a few farms scattered along at different elevations, each commanding a fine prospect of the mountains to the north, and a stream ran down the middle of the valley on which near the head there was a mill. It seemed a road for the pilgrim to enter upon who would climb to the gates of heaven. Now I crossed a hayfield, and now over the brook on a slight bridge, still gradually ascending all the while with a sort of awe, and filled with indefinite expectations as to what kind of inhabitants and what kind of nature I should come to at last. It now seemed some advantage that the earth was uneven, for one could not imagine a more noble position for a farm-house than this vale afforded, farther from or nearer to its head, from a glen-like seclusion overlooking the country at a great elevation between these two mountain walls.

It reminded me of the homesteads of the Huguenots, on Staten Island, off the coast of New Jersey. The hills in the interior of this island, though comparatively low, are penetrated in various directions by similar sloping valleys on a humble scale, gradually narrowing and rising at the centre, and at the head of these the Huguenots, who were the first settlers, placed their houses quite within the land, in rural and sheltered places, in leafy recesses where the breeze played with the poplar and the gum-tree, from which, with equal security in calm and storm, they looked out through a widening vista, over miles of forest and stretching salt marsh, to the Huguenot's Tree, an old elm on the shore, at whose root they had landed, and across the spacious outer bay of New York to Sandy Hook and the Highlands of Neversink, and thence over leagues of the Atlantic, perchance to some faint vessel in the horizon, almost a day's sail on her voyage to that Europe whence they had come.

When walking in the interior there, in the midst of rural scenery, where there was as little to remind me of the ocean as amid the New Hampshire hills, I have suddenly, through a gap, a cleft or "clove road," as the Dutch settlers called it, caught sight of a ship under full sail, over a field of corn, twenty or thirty miles at sea. The effect was similar, since I had no means of measuring distances, to seeing a painted ship passed backwards and forwards through a magic lantern.

But to return to the mountain. It seemed as if he must be the most singular and heavenly minded man whose dwelling stood highest up the valley. The thunder had rumbled at my heels all the way, but the shower passed off in another direction, though if it had not, I half believed that I should get above it. I at length reached the last house but one, where the path to the summit diverged to the right, while the summit itself rose directly in front. But I determined to follow up the valley to its head, and then find my own route up the steep as the shorter and more adventurous way. I had thoughts of returning to this house, which was well kept and so nobly placed, the next day, and perhaps remaining a week there, if I could have entertainment.

Its mistress was a frank and hospitable young woman, who stood before me in a dishabille, busily and unconcernedly combing her long black hair while she talked, giving her head the necessary toss with each sweep of the comb, with lively, sparkling eyes, and full of interest in that lower world from which I had come, talking all the while as familiarly as if she had known me for years, and reminding me of a cousin of mine. She at first had taken me for a student from Williamstown, for they went by in parties, she said, either riding or walking, almost every pleasant day, and were a pretty wild set of fellows; but they never went by the way I was going.

As I passed the last house, a man called out to know what I had to sell, for, seeing my knapsack, he thought that I might be a peddler who was taking this unusual route over the ridge of the valley into South Adams. He told me that it was still four or five miles to the summit by the path which I had left, though not more than two in a straight line from where I was, but that nobody ever went this way; there was no path, and I should find it as steep as the roof of a house. But I knew that I was more used to the woods and mountains than he, and went along through his cow-yard, while he, looking at the sun, shouted after me that I should not get to the top that night.

I soon reached the head of the valley, but as I could not see the summit from this point, I ascended a low

mountain on the opposite side, and took its bearing with my compass. I at once entered the woods, and began to climb the steep side of the mountain in a diagonal direction, taking the bearing of a tree every dozen rods. The ascent was by no means difficult or unpleasant, and occupied much less time than it would have taken to follow the path.

Even country people, I have observed, magnify the difficulty of traveling in the forest, and especially among mountains. They seem to lack their usual common sense in this. I have climbed several higher mountains without guide or path, and have found, as might be expected, that it takes only more time and patience commonly than to travel the smoothest highway. It is very rare that you meet with obstacles in this world which the humblest man has not faculties to surmount. It is true we may come to a perpendicular precipice, but we need not jump off, nor run our heads against it. A man may jump down his own cellar stairs, or dash his brains out against his chimney, if he is mad.

So far as my experience goes, travelers generally exaggerate the difficulties of the way. Like most evil, the difficulty is imaginary; for what's the hurry? If a person lost would conclude that after all he is not lost, he is not beside himself, but standing in his own old shoes on the very spot where he is, and that for the time being he will live there; but the places that have known him, *they* are lost, — how much anxiety and danger would vanish. I am not alone if I stand by myself. Who knows where in space this globe is rolling? Yet we will not give ourselves up for lost, let it go where it will.

I made my way steadily upward in a straight line, through a dense undergrowth of mountain laurel, until the trees began to have a scraggy and infernal look, as if contending with frost goblins, and at length I reached the summit, just as the sun was setting. Several acres here had been cleared, and were covered with rocks and stumps, and there was a rude observatory in the middle which overlooked the woods. I had one fair view of the country before the sun went down, but I was too thirsty to waste any light in viewing the prospect, and set out directly to find water.

First, going down a well-beaten path for half a mile through the low scrubby wood, till I came to where the water stood in the tracks of the horses which had carried travelers up, I lay down flat, and drank these dry, one after another, a pure, cold, spring-like water, but yet I could not fill my dipper, though I contrived little siphons of grass-stems, and ingenious aqueducts on a small scale; it was too slow a process. Then, remembering that I had passed a moist place near the top, on my way up, I returned to find it again, and here, with sharp stones and my hands, in the twilight, I made a well about two feet deep, which was soon filled with pure cold water, and the birds too came and drank at it. So I filled my dipper, and, making my way back to the observatory, collected some dry sticks, and made a fire on some flat stones which had been placed on the floor for that purpose, and so I soon cooked my supper of rice, having already whittled a wooden spoon to eat it with.

I sat up during the evening, reading by the light of the fire the scraps of newspapers in which some party had wrapped their luncheon; the prices current in New York and Boston, the advertisements, and the singular editorials which some had seen fit to publish, not foreseeing under what critical circumstances they would be read. I read these things at a vast advantage there, and it seemed to me that the advertisements, or what is called the business part of a paper, were greatly the best, the most useful, natural, and respectable.

Almost all the opinions and sentiments expressed were so little considered, so shallow and flimsy, that I thought the very texture of the paper must be weaker in that part and tear the more easily. The advertisements and the prices current were more closely allied to nature, and were respectable in some measure as tide and meteorological tables are; but the reading-matter, which I remembered was most prized down below, unless it was some humble record of science, or an extract from some old classic, struck me as strangely whimsical, and crude, and one-idea'd, like a school-boy's theme, such as youths write and after burn. The opinions were of that kind that are doomed to wear a different aspect to-morrow, like last year's fashions; as if mankind were very green indeed, and would be ashamed of themselves in a few years, when they had outgrown this verdant period. There was, moreover, a singular disposition to wit and humor, but rarely the slightest real success; and the apparent success was a terrible satire on the attempt; the Evil Genius of man laughed the loudest at his best jokes.

The advertisements, as I have said, such as were serious, and not of the modern quack kind, suggested pleasing and poetic thoughts; for commerce is really as interesting as nature. The very names of the commodities were poetic, and as suggestive as if they had been inserted in a pleasing poem, — Lumber, Cotton, Sugar, Hides, Guano, Logwood. Some sober, private, and original thought would have been grateful to read there, and as much in harmony with the circumstances as if it had been written on a mountain-top; for it is of a fashion which never changes, and as respectable as hides and logwood, or any natural product. What an inestimable companion such a scrap of paper would have been, containing some fruit of a mature life! What a relic! What a recipe! It seemed a divine invention, by which not mere shining coin, but shining and current thoughts, could be brought up and left there.

As it was cold, I collected quite a pile of wood and lay down on a board against the side of the building, not having any blanket to cover me, with my head to the fire, that I might look after it, which is not the Indian rule. But as it grew colder towards midnight, I at length encased myself completely in boards, managing even to put a board on top of me, with a large stone on it, to keep it down, and so slept comfortably. I was reminded, it is true, of the Irish children, who inquired what their neighbors did who had no door to put over them in winter nights as they had; but I am convinced that there was nothing very strange in the inquiry. Those who have never tried it can have no idea how far a door, which keeps the single blanket down, may go toward making one comfortable.

We are constituted a good deal like chickens, which, taken from the hen, and put in a basket of cotton in the chimney-corner, will often peep till they die, nevertheless; but if you put in a book, or anything heavy, which will press down the cotton, and feel like the hen, they go to sleep directly. My only companions were the mice, which came up to pick up the crumbs that had been left in those scraps of paper; still, as everywhere, pensioners on man, and not unwisely improving this elevated tract for their habitation. They nibbled what was for them; I nibbled what was for me. Once or twice in the night, when I looked up, I saw a white cloud drifting through the windows, and filling the whole upper story.

This observatory was a building of considerable size, erected by the students of Williamstown College, whose buildings might be seen by daylight gleaming far down in the valley. It would be no small advantage if every college were thus located at the base of a mountain, as good at least as one well-endowed professorship. It were as well to be educated in the shadow of a mountain as in more classical shades. Some will remember, no doubt, not only that they went to the college, but that they went to the mountain. Every visit to its summit would, as it were, generalize the particular information gained below, and subject it to more catholic tests.

I was up early and perched upon the top of this tower to see the daybreak, for some time reading the names

that had been engraved there, before I could distinguish more distant objects.[1] An "untamable fly" buzzed at my elbow with the same nonchalance as on on a molasses hogshead at the end of Long Wharf. Even there I must attend to his stale humdrum. But now I come to the pith of this long digression. As the light increased, I discovered around me an ocean of mist, which by chance reached up exactly to the base of the tower, and shut out every vestige of the earth, while I was left floating on this fragment of the wreck of a world, on my carved plank, in cloudland; a situation which required no aid from the imagination to render it impressive.

---

[1] This old wooden tower has been replaced by a granite memorial tower dedicated to the soldiers and sailors of Massachusetts.

As the light in the east steadily increased, it revealed to me more clearly the new world into which I had risen in the night, the new *terra firma* perchance of my future life. There was not a crevice left through which the trivial places we name Massachusetts or Vermont or New York could be seen, while I still inhaled the clear atmosphere of a July morning, — if it were July there. All around beneath me was spread for a hundred miles on every side, as far as the eye could reach, an undulating country of clouds, answering in the varied swell of its surface to the terrestrial world it veiled.

It was such a country as we might see in dreams, with all the delights of paradise. There were immense snowy pastures, apparently smooth shaven and firm, and shady vales between the vaporous mountains; and far in the horizon I could see where some luxurious misty timber jutted into the prairie, and trace the windings of a watercourse, some unimagined Amazon or Orinoko, by the misty trees on its brink. As there was wanting the symbol, so there was not the substance of impurity, no spot nor stain. It was a favor for which to be forever silent to be shown this vision.

The earth beneath had become such a flitting thing of lights and shadows as the clouds had been before. It was not merely veiled to me, but it had passed away like the phantom of a shadow, *σκιᾶς ὄναρ*, and this new platform was gained. As I had climbed above storm and cloud, so by successive days' journeys I might reach the region of eternal day, beyond the tapering shadow of the earth.

But when its own sun began to rise on this pure world, I found myself a dweller in the dazzling halls of Aurora, into which poets have had but a partial glance over the eastern hills, drifting amid the saffron-colored clouds, and playing with the rosy fingers of the Dawn, in the very path of the Sun's chariot, and sprinkled with its dewy dust, enjoying the benignant smile, and near at hand the far-darting glances of the god. The inhabitants of earth behold commonly but the dark and shadowy under side of heaven's pavement; it is only when seen at a favorable angle in the horizon, morning or evening, that some faint streaks of the rich lining of the clouds are revealed. But my muse would fail to convey an impression of the gorgeous tapestry by which I was surrounded, such as men see faintly reflected afar off in the chambers of the east.

Here, as on earth, I saw the gracious god "Flatter the mountain-tops with sovereign eye . . . Gilding pale streams with heavenly alchemy." But never here did "Heaven's sun" stain himself.

But, alas, owing, as I think, to some unworthiness in myself, my private sun did stain himself, and "Anon permit the basest clouds to ride With ugly wrack on his celestial face"—for before the god had reached the zenith the heavenly pavement rose and embraced my wavering virtue, or rather I sank down again into that "forlorn world," from which the celestial sun had hid his visage.

In the preceding evening I had seen the summits of new and yet higher mountains, the Catskills, by which I might hope to climb to heaven again, and had set my compass for a fair lake in the southwest, which lay in my way, for which I now steered, descending the mountain by my own route, on the side opposite to that by which I had ascended, and soon found myself in the region of cloud and drizzling rain, and the inhabitants affirmed that it had been a cloudy and drizzling day wholly.

But now we must make haste back before the fog disperses to the blithe Merrimack water. We passed a canal-boat before sunrise, groping its way to the seaboard, and, though we could not see it on account of the fog, the few dull, thumping, stertorous sounds which we heard impressed us with a sense of weight and irresistible motion. One little rill of commerce already awake on this distant New Hampshire river. The fog, as it required more skill in the steering, enhanced the interest of our early voyage, and made the river seem indefinitely broad. A slight mist, through which objects are faintly visible, has the effect of expanding even ordinary streams, by a singular mirage, into arms of the sea or inland lakes. In the present instance, it was even fragrant and invigorating, and we enjoyed it as a sort of earlier sunshine, or dewy and embryo light.

The same pleasant and observant historian whom we quoted above says that, "In the mountainous parts of the country, the ascent of vapors, and their formation into clouds, is a curious and entertaining object. The vapors are seen rising in small columns like smoke from many chimneys. When risen to a certain height, they spread, meet, condense, and are attracted to the mountains, where they either distill in gentle dews, and replenish the springs, or descend in showers, accompanied with thunder. After short intermissions, the process is repeated many times in the course of a summer day, affording to travelers a lively illustration of what is observed in the Book of Job, 'They are wet with the showers of the mountains.'"

Fogs and clouds which conceal the overshadowing mountains lend the breadth of the plains to mountain vales. Even a small-featured country acquires some grandeur in stormy weather when clouds are seen drifting between the beholder and the neighboring hills. When, in traveling toward Haverhill through Hampstead in this State, on the height of land between the Merrimack and the Piscataqua or the sea, you commence the descent eastward, the view toward the coast is so distant and unexpected, though the sea is invisible, that you at first suppose the unobstructed atmosphere to be a fog in the lowlands concealing hills of corresponding elevation to that you are upon; but it is the mist of prejudice alone, which the winds will not disperse.

The most stupendous scenery ceases to be sublime when it becomes distinct, or in other words limited, and the imagination is no longer encouraged to exaggerate it. The actual height and breadth of a mountain or a waterfall are always ridiculously small; they are the imagined only that content us. Nature is not made after such a fashion as we would have her. We piously exaggerate her wonders, as the scenery around our home.

Such was the heaviness of the dews along this river that we were generally obliged to leave our tent spread over the bows of the boat till the sun had dried it, to avoid mildew. We passed the mouth of Penichook Brook, a wild salmon-stream, in the fog, without seeing it. At length the sun's rays struggled through the mist and showed us the pines on shore dripping with dew, and springs trickling from the moist banks. We rowed for some hours between glistening banks before the sun had dried the grass and leaves, or the day had established its character. Its serenity at last seemed the more profound and secure for the denseness of the morning's fog.

The river became swifter, and the scenery more pleasing than before. The banks were steep and clayey for the most part, and trickling with water, and where a spring oozed out a few feet above the river the boatmen had cut a trough out of a slab with their axes, and placed it so as to receive the water and fill their jugs conveniently. Sometimes this purer and cooler water, bursting out from under a pine or a rock, was collected into a basin close to the edge of and level with the river, a fountainhead of the Merrimack. So near along life's stream are the fountains of innocence and youth making fertile its sandy margin; and the voyageur will do well to replenish his vessels often at these uncontaminated sources. Some youthful spring, perchance, still empties with tinkling music into the oldest river, even when it is falling into the sea, and we imagine that its music is distinguished by the river-gods from the general lapse of the stream, and falls sweeter on their ears in proportion as it is nearer to the ocean. As the evaporations of the river feed thus these unsuspected springs which filter through its banks, so, perchance, our aspirations fall back again in springs on the margin of life's stream to refresh and purify it. The yellow and tepid river may float his scow, and cheer his eye with its reflections and its ripples, but the boatman quenches his thirst at this small rill alone. It is this purer and cooler element that chiefly sustains his life. The race will long survive that is thus discreet.

Our course this morning lay between the territories of Merrimack, on the west, and Litchfield, once called Brenton's Farm, on the east, which townships were anciently the Indian Naticook. Brenton was a fur-trader among the Indians, and these lands were granted to him in 1656. The latter township contains about five hundred inhabitants, of whom, however, we saw none, and but few of their dwellings. Being on the river, whose banks are always high and generally conceal the few houses, the country appeared much more wild and primitive than to the traveler on the neighboring roads. The river is by far the most attractive highway, and those boatmen who have spent twenty or twenty-five years on it must have had a much fairer, more wild, and memorable experience than the dusty and jarring one of the teamster who has driven, during the same time, on the roads which run parallel with the stream. As one ascends the Merrimack he rarely sees a village, but for the most part alternate wood and pasture lands, and sometimes a field of corn or potatoes, of rye or oats or English grass, with a few straggling apple-trees, and, at still longer intervals, a farmer's house. The soil, excepting the best of the intervale, is commonly as light and sandy as a patriot could desire. Sometimes this forenoon the country appeared in its primitive state, and as if the Indian still inhabited it, and, again, as if many free, new settlers occupied it, their slight fences straggling down to the water's edge; and the barking of dogs, and even the prattle of children, were heard, and smoke was seen to go up from some hearthstone, and the banks were divided into patches of pasture, mowing, tillage, and woodland.

But when the river spread out broader, with an uninhabited islet, or a long, low, sandy shore which ran on single and devious, not answering to its opposite, but far off as if it were sea-shore or single coast, and the land no longer nursed the river in its bosom, but they conversed as equals, the rustling leaves with rippling waves, and few fences were seen, but high oak woods on one side, and large herds of cattle, and all tracks seemed a point to one centre behind some statelier grove, — we imagined that the river flowed through an extensive manor, and that the few inhabitants were retainers to a lord, and a feudal state of things prevailed.

When there was a suitable reach, we caught sight of the Goffstown mountain, the Indian Uncannunuc, rising before us on the west side. It was a calm and beautiful day, with only a slight zephyr to ripple the surface of the water, and rustle the woods on shore, and just warmth enough to prove the kindly disposition of Nature to her children. With buoyant spirits and vigorous impulses we tossed our boat rapidly along into the very middle of this forenoon. The fish-hawk sailed and screamed overhead.

The chipping or striped squirrel, *Sciurus striatus* (*Tamius Lysteri*, Aud.), sat upon the end of some Virginia fence or rider reaching over the stream, twirling a green nut with one paw, as in a lathe, while the other held it fast against its incisors as chisels. Like an independent russet leaf, with a will of its own, rustling whither it could;

now under the fence, now over it, now peeping at the voyageurs through a crack with only its tail visible, now at its lunch deep in the toothsome kernel, and now a rod off playing at hide-and-seek, with the nut stowed away in its chops, where were half a dozen more besides, extending its cheeks to a ludicrous breadth, — as if it were devising through what safe valve of frisk or somerset to let its superfluous life escape; the stream passing harmlessly off, even while it sits, in constant electric flashes through its tail. And now with a chuckling squeak it dives into the root of a hazel, and we see no more of it.

Or the larger red squirrel or chickaree, sometimes called the Hudson Bay squirrel (*Sciurus Hudsonius*), gave warning of our approach by that peculiar alarum of his, like the winding up of some strong clock, in the top of a pine-tree, and dodged behind its stem, or leaped from tree to tree with such caution and adroitness, as if much depended on the fidelity of his scout, running along the white-pine boughs sometimes twenty rods by our side, with such speed, and by such unerring routes, as if it were some well-worn familiar path to him; and presently, when we have passed, he returns to his work of cutting off the pine-cones, and letting them fall to the ground.

We passed Cromwell's Falls, the first we met with on this river, this forenoon, by means of locks, without using our wheels.[1] These falls are the Nesenkeag of the Indians.

---

[1] These falls — Cromwell's and farther upstream, Moore's, Coo's, Goff's, Short's and Griffith's — all of which they passed by means of

Great Nesenkeag Stream comes in on the right just above, and Little Nesenkeag some distance below, both in Litchfield. We read in the Gazetteer, under the head of Merrimack, that

"The first house in this town was erected on the margin of the river [soon after 1665] for a house of traffic with the Indians. For some time one Cromwell carried on a lucrative trade with them, weighing their furs with his foot, till, enraged at his supposed or real deception, they formed the resolution to murder him. This intention being communicated to Cromwell, he buried his wealth and made his escape. Within a few hours after his flight, a party of the Penacook tribe arrived, and, not finding the object of their resentment, burnt his habitation."

Upon the top of the high bank here, close to the river, was still to be seen his cellar, now overgrown with trees. It was a convenient spot for such a traffic, at the foot of the first falls above the settlements, and commanding a pleasant view up the river, where he could see the Indians coming down with their furs. The lockman told us that his shovel and tongs had been ploughed up here, and also a stone with his name on it. But we will not vouch for the truth of this story. In the New Hampshire His-

---

locks, are prominently featured on the maps of the period, as becomes landmarks important in an era of water-borne commerce. Today not one of them appears by name in the current issue of the *United States Geological Survey* "Topographic Map" of this area — Manchester Quadrangle. Their location in the end-paper maps has been established from the text and by reference to contemporary sources.

torical Collections for 1815 it says, "Some time after, pewter was found in the well, and an iron pot and trammel in the sand; the latter are preserved." These were the traces of the white trader. On the opposite bank, where it jutted over the stream cape-wise, we picked up four arrow-heads, and a small Indian tool made of stone, as soon as we had climbed it, where plainly there had once stood a wigwam of the Indians with whom Cromwell traded, and who fished and hunted here before he came.

As usual, the gossips have not been silent respecting Cromwell's buried wealth, and it is said that some years ago a farmer's plough, not far from here, slid over a flat stone which emitted a hollow sound, and, on its being raised, a small hole six inches in diameter was discovered, stoned about, from which a sum of money was taken. The lock-man told us another similar story about a farmer in a neighboring town, who had been a poor man, but who suddenly bought a good farm, and was well to do in the world, and, when he was questioned, did not give a satisfactory account of the matter; how few, alas, could! This caused his hired man to remember that one day, as they were ploughing together, the plough struck something, and his employer, going back to look, concluded not to go round again, saying that the sky looked rather lowering, and so put up his team. The like urgency has caused many things to be remembered which never transpired. The truth is, there is money buried everywhere, and you have only to go to work to find it.

Not far from these falls stands an oak-tree, on the intervale, about a quarter of a mile from the river, on the farm of a Mr. Lund, which was pointed out to us as the spot where French, the leader of the party which went in pursuit of the Indians from Dunstable, was killed. Farwell dodged them in the thick woods near. It did not look as if men had ever had to run for their lives on this now open and peaceful intervale.

Here too was another extensive desert by the side of the road in Litchfield, visible from the bank of the river. The sand was blown off in some places to the depth of ten or twelve feet, leaving small grotesque hillocks of that height, where there was a clump of bushes firmly rooted. Thirty or forty years ago, as we were told, it was a sheep-pasture, but the sheep, being worried by the fleas, began to paw the ground, till they broke the sod, and so the sand began to blow, till now it had extended over forty or fifty acres. This evil might easily have been remedied, at first, by spreading birches with their leaves on over the sand, and fastening them down with stakes, to break the wind. The fleas bit the sheep, and the sheep bit the ground, and the sore had spread to this extent.

It is astonishing what a great sore a little scratch breedeth. Who knows but Sahara, where caravans and cities are buried, began with the bite of an African flea? This poor globe, how it must itch in many places! Will no god be kind enough to spread a salve of birches over its sores?

Here too we noticed where the Indians had gathered a heap of stones, perhaps for their council-fire, which by their weight having prevented the sand under them from blowing away, were left on the summit of a mound. They told us that arrowheads, and also bullets of lead and iron, had been found here.

We noticed several other sandy tracts in our voyage; and the course of the Merrimack can be traced from the nearest mountain by its yellow sand-banks, though the river itself is for the most part invisible. Lawsuits, as we hear, have in some cases grown out of these causes. Railroads have been made through certain irritable districts, breaking their sod, and so have set the sand to blowing, till it has converted fertile farms into deserts, and the company has had to pay the damages.

This sand seemed to us the connecting link between land and water. It was a kind of water on which you could walk, and you could see the ripple-marks on its surface, produced by the winds, precisely like those at the bottom of a brook or lake. We had read that Mussulmans are permitted by the Koran to perform their ablutions in sand when they cannot get water, a necessary indulgence in Arabia, and we now understood the propriety of this provision.

Plum Island, at the mouth of this river, to whose formation, perhaps, these very banks have sent their contribution, is a similar desert of drifting sand, of various colors, blown into graceful curves by the wind. It is a mere sand-bar exposed, stretching nine miles parallel to the coast, and, exclusive of the marsh on the inside, rarely more than half a mile wide. There are but half a dozen houses on it, and it is almost without a tree, or a sod, or any green thing with which a countryman is familiar. The thin vegetation stands half buried in sand, as in drifting snow. The only shrub, the beach-plum, which gives the island its name, grows but a few feet high; but this is so abundant that parties of a hundred at once come from the main-land and down the Merrimack, in September, pitch their tents, and gather the plums, which are good to eat raw and to preserve.

The graceful and delicate beach-pea, too, grows abundantly amid the sand, and several strange, moss-like and succulent plants. The island for its whole length is scolloped into low hills, not more than twenty feet high, by the wind, and, excepting a faint trail on the edge of the marsh, is as trackless as Sahara. There are dreary bluffs of sand and valleys ploughed by the wind, where you might expect to discover the bones of a caravan. Schooners come from Boston to load with the sand for masons' uses, and in a few hours the wind obliterates all traces of their work. Yet you have only to dig a foot or two anywhere to come to fresh water; and you are surprised to learn that woodchucks abound here, and foxes are found, though you see not where they can burrow or hide themselves.

I have walked down the whole length of its broad

beach at low tide, at which time alone you can find a firm ground to walk on, and probably Massachusetts does not furnish a more grand and dreary walk. On the seaside there are only a distant sail and a few coots to break the grand monotony. A solitary stake stuck up, or a sharper sand-hill than usual, is remarkable as a landmark for miles; while for music you hear only the ceaseless sound of the surf, and the dreary peep of the beach-birds.[1]

There were several canal-boats at Cromwell's Falls passing through the locks, for which we waited. In the forward part of one stood a brawny New Hampshire man, leaning on his pole, bareheaded and in shirt and trousers only, a rude Apollo of a man, coming down from that "vast uplandish country," to the main; of nameless age, with flaxen hair, and vigorous, weather-bleached countenance, in whose wrinkles the sun still lodged, as little touched by the heats and frosts and withering cares of life as a maple of the mountain; an undressed, unkempt, uncivil man, with whom we parleyed awhile, and parted not without a sincere interest in one another. His humanity was genuine and instinctive, and his rudeness only a manner. He inquired, just as we were passing out of earshot, if we had killed anything, and we shouted after him

---

[1] The time would come when Thoreau would revise this view of the unique aspect of Plum Island Beach. And some years later following his excursions to Cape Cod, he did. There, in company with the poet William Ellery Channing and alone, he several times in the 1850's traversed the great outer beach on that "bared and bended arm of Massachusetts. . . . A man may stand there and put all America behind him." *Cape Cod,* N.Y. 1951.

that we had shot a *buoy*, and could see him for a long while scratching his head in vain to know if he had heard aright.

There is reason in the distinction of civil and uncivil. The manners are sometimes so rough a rind that we doubt whether they cover any core or sap-wood at all. We sometimes meet uncivil men, children of Amazons, who dwell by mountain paths, and are said to be inhospitable to strangers, whose salutation is as rude as the grasp of their brawny hands, and who deal with men as unceremoniously as they are wont to deal with the elements. They need only to extend their clearings, and let in more sunlight, to seek out the southern slopes of the hills, from which they may look down on the civil plain or ocean, and temper their diet duly with the cereal fruits, consuming less wild meat and acorns, to become like the inhabitants of cities. A true politeness does not result from any hasty and artificial polishing, it is true, but grows naturally in characters of the right grain and quality, through a long fronting of men and events, and rubbing on good and bad fortune. Perhaps I can tell a tale to the purpose while the lock is filling, — for our voyage this forenoon furnishes but few incidents of importance.

Early one summer morning I had left the shores of the Connecticut, and for the livelong day traveled up the bank of a river, which came in from the west; now looking down on the stream, foaming and rippling through the forest a mile off, from the hills over which the road led, and now sitting on its rocky brink and dipping my feet in its rapids, or bathing adventurously in mid-channel. The hills grew more and more frequent, and gradually swelled into mountains as I advanced, hemming in the course of the river, so that at last I could not see where it came from, and was at liberty to imagine the most wonderful meanderings and descents. At noon I slept on the grass in the shade of a maple, where the river had found a broader channel than usual, and was spread out shallow, with frequent sand-bars exposed. In the names of the towns I recognized some which I had long ago read on teamsters' wagons, that had come from far up country; quiet uplandish towns, of mountainous fame.

I walked along, musing and enchanted, by rows of sugar-maples, through the small and uninquisitive villages, and sometimes was pleased with the sight of a boat drawn up on a sand-bar, where there appeared no inhabitants to use it. It seemed, however, as essential to the river as a fish, and to lend a certain dignity to it. It was like the trout of mountain streams to the fishes of the sea, or like the young of the land-crab born far in the interior, who have never yet heard the sound of the ocean's surf. The hills approached nearer and nearer to the stream, until at last they closed behind me, and I found myself just before nightfall in a romantic and retired valley, about half a mile in length, and barely wide enough for the stream at its bottom. I thought that there could be no finer site for a cottage among mountains. You could anywhere run across the stream on the rocks, and its constant murmuring would quiet the passions of mankind forever.

Suddenly the road, which seemed aiming for the mountain-side, turned short to the left, and another valley opened, concealing the former, and of the same character with it. It was the most remarkable and pleasing scenery I had ever seen. I found here a few mild and hospitable inhabitants, who, as the day was not quite spent, and I was anxious to improve the light, directed me four or five miles farther on my way to the dwelling of a man whose name was Rice, who occupied the last and highest of the valleys that lay in my path, and who, they said, was a rather rude and uncivil man. But "what is a foreign country to those who have science? Who is a stranger to those who have the habit of speaking kindly?"

At length, as the sun was setting behind the mountains in a still darker and more solitary vale, I reached the dwelling of this man. Except for the narrowness of the plain, and that the stones were solid granite, it was the counterpart of that retreat to which Belphoebe bore the wounded Timias.

I observed, as I drew near, that he was not so rude as I had anticipated, for he kept many cattle, and dogs to watch them, and I saw where he had made maple-sugar on the sides of the mountains, and above all distinguished the voices of children mingling with the murmur of the torrent before the door. As I passed his stable, I met one whom I supposed to be a hired man, attending to his cattle, and I inquired if they entertained travelers at that house. "Sometimes we do," he answered gruffly, and immediately went to the farthest stall from me, and I perceived that it was Rice himself whom I had addressed. But pardoning this incivility to the wildness of the scenery, I bent my steps to the house.

There was no sign-post before it, nor any of the usual invitations to the traveler, though I saw by the road that many went and came there, but the owner's name only was fastened to the outside; a sort of implied and sullen invitation, as I thought. I passed from room to room without meeting any one, till I came to what seemed the guests' apartment, which was neat, and even had an air of refinement about it, and I was glad to find a map against the wall which would direct me on my journey on the morrow. At length I heard a step in a distant apartment, which was the first I had entered, and went to see if the landlord had come in; but it proved to be only a child, one of those whose voices I had heard, probably his son, and between him and me stood in the doorway a large watch-dog, which growled at me, and looked as if he would presently spring, but the boy did not speak to him; and when I asked for a glass of water, he briefly said, "It runs in the corner." So I took a mug from the counter and went out of doors, and searched round the corner of the house, but could find neither well nor spring, nor any water but the stream which ran all along the front. I came back, therefore, and, setting down the mug, asked the child if the stream was good to drink; whereupon he seized the mug, and, going to the corner of the room, where a cool spring which issued from the mountain behind trickled through a pipe into the apartment, filled it, and drank, and gave it to me empty again, and, calling to the dog, rushed out of doors.

Erelong some of the hired men made their appearance, and drank at the spring, and lazily washed themselves and combed their hair in silence, and some sat down as if weary, and fell asleep in their seats. But all the while I saw no women, though I sometimes heard a bustle in that part of the house from which the spring came. At length, Rice himself came in, for it was now dark, with an ox-whip in his hand, breathing hard, and he too soon settled down into his seat not far from me, as if, now that his day's work was done, he had no farther to travel, but only to digest his supper at his leisure.

When I asked him if he could give me a bed, he said there was one ready, in such a tone as implied that I ought to have known it, and the less said about that the better. So far so good. And yet he continued to look at me as if he would fain have me say something further like a traveler. I remarked that it was a wild and rugged country he inhabited, and worth coming many miles to see. "Not so very rough neither," said he, and appealed to his men to bear witness to the breadth and smoothness of his fields, which consisted in all of one small intervale, and to the size of his crops; "and if we have some hills," added he, "there's no better pasturage anywhere."

I then asked if this place was the one I had heard of, calling it by a name I had seen on the map, or if it was a certain other; and he answered, gruffly, that it was neither the one nor the other; that he had settled it and cultivated it, and made it what it was, and I could know nothing about it. Observing some guns and other implements of hunting hanging on brackets around the room, and his hounds now sleeping on the floor, I took occasion to change the discourse, and inquired if there was much game in that country, and he answered this question more graciously, having some glimmering of my drift; but when I inquired if there were any bears, he answered impatiently that he was no more in danger of losing his sheep than his neighbors; he had tamed and civilized that region.

After a pause, thinking of my journey on the morrow, and the few hours of daylight in that hollow and mountainous country, which would require me to be on my way betimes, I remarked that the day must be shorter by an hour there than on the neighboring plains; at which he gruffly asked what I knew about it, and affirmed that he had as much daylight as his neighbors; he ventured to say, the days were longer there than where I lived, as I should find if I stayed; that in some way, I could not be expected to understand how, the sun came over the mountains half an hour earlier, and stayed half an hour later there than on the neighboring plains. And more of like sort he said.

He was, indeed, as rude as a fabled satyr. But I suffered him to pass for what he was, — for why should I quarrel with nature? — and was even pleased at the discovery of such a singular natural phenomenon. I dealt with him as if to me all manners were indifferent, and he had a sweet, wild way with him. I would not question nature, and I would rather have him as he was than as I would have him. For I had come up here not for sympathy, or kindness, or society, but for novelty and adventure, and to see what nature had produced here. I therefore did not repel his rudeness, but quite innocently welcomed it all, and knew how to appreciate it, as if I were reading in an old drama a part well sustained. He was indeed a coarse and sensual man, and, as I have said, uncivil, but he had his just quarrel with nature and mankind, I have no doubt, only he had no artificial covering to his ill-humors. He was earthy enough, but yet there was good soil in him, and even a long-suffering Saxon probity at bottom. If you could represent the case to him, he would not let the race die out in him, like a red Indian.

At length I told him that he was a fortunate man, and I trusted that he was grateful for so much light; and, rising, said I would take a lamp, and that I would pay him then for my lodging, for I expected to recommence my journey even as early as the sun rose in his country; but he answered in haste, and this time civilly, that I should not fail to find some of his household stirring, however early, for they were no sluggards, and I could take my breakfast with them before I started, if I chose; and as he lighted the lamp I detected a gleam of true hospitality and ancient civility, a beam of pure and even gentle humanity, from his bleared and moist eyes. It was a look more intimate with me, and more explanatory, than any words of his could have been if he had tried to his dying day.

It was more significant than any Rice of those parts could even comprehend, and long anticipated this man's culture, — a glance of his pure genius, which did not much enlighten him, but did impress and rule him for the moment, and faintly constrain his voice and manner. He cheerfully led the way to my apartment, stepping over the limbs of his men, who were asleep on the floor in an intervening chamber, and showed me a clean and comfortable bed. For many pleasant hours after the household was asleep I sat at the open window, for it was a sultry night, and heard the little river. But I arose as usual by starlight the next morning, before my host, or his men, or even his dogs, were awake; and, having left a ninepence on the counter, was already half-way over the mountain with the sun before they had broken their fast.

Before I had left the country of my host, while the first rays of the sun slanted over the mountains, as I stopped by the wayside to gather some raspberries, a very old

man, not far from a hundred, came along with a milking-pail in his hand, and turning aside began to pluck the berries near me. When I inquired the way, he answered in a low, rough voice, without looking up or seeming to regard my presence, which I imputed to his years; and presently, muttering to himself, he proceeded to collect his cows in a neighboring pasture; and when he had again returned near to the wayside, he suddenly stopped, while his cows went on before, and, uncovering his head, prayed aloud in the cool morning air, as if he had forgotten this exercise before, for his daily bread, and also that He who letteth his rain fall on the just and on the unjust, and without whom not a sparrow falleth to the ground, would not neglect the stranger (meaning me), and with even more direct and personal applications, though mainly according to the long-established formula common to lowlanders and the inhabitants of mountains.

When he had done praying, I made bold to ask him if

he had any cheese in his hut which he would sell me, but he answered without looking up, and in the same low and repulsive voice as before, that they did not make any, and went to milking. It is written, "The stranger who turneth away from a house with disappointed hopes, leaveth there his own offenses, and departeth, taking with him all the good actions of the owner."

Being now fairly in the stream of this week's commerce, we began to meet with boats more frequently, and hailed them from time to time with the freedom of sailors. The boatmen appeared to lead an easy and contented life, and we thought that we should prefer their employment ourselves to many professions which are much more sought after. They suggested how few circumstances are necessary to the well-being and serenity of man, how indifferent all employments are, and that any may seem noble and poetic to the eyes of men, if pursued with sufficient buoyancy and freedom. With liberty and pleasant weather, the simplest occupation, any unquestioned country mode of life which detains us in the open air, is alluring. The man who picks peas steadily for a living is more than respectable, he is even envied by his shop-worn neighbors. We are as happy as the birds when our Good Genius permits us to pursue any outdoor work, without a sense of dissipation. Our penknife glitters in the sun; our voice is echoed by yonder wood; if an oar drops, we are fain to let it drop again.

The canal-boat is of very simple construction, requiring but little ship-timber, and, as we were told, costs about two hundred dollars. They are managed by two men. In ascending the stream they use poles fourteen or fifteen feet long, pointed with iron, walking about one third the length of the boat from the forward end. Going down, they commonly keep in the middle of the stream, using an oar at each end; or if the wind is favorable they raise their broad sail, and have only to steer.[1] They commonly carry down wood or bricks, — fifteen or sixteen cords of wood, and as many thousand bricks, at a time, — and bring back stores for the country, consuming two or three days each way between Concord and Charlestown. They sometimes pile the wood so as to leave a shelter in one part where they may retire from the rain.

One can hardly imagine a more healthful employment, or one more favorable to contemplation and the observation of nature. Unlike the mariner, they have the constantly varying panorama of the shore to relieve the monotony of their labor, and it seemed to us that as they thus glided noiselessly from town to town, with all their furniture about them, for their very homestead is a movable, they could comment on the character of the inhab-

[1] Thoreau's description fits that of the gundalow, that double-ended flat-bottomed scow so long in use on the salt rivers and marshes of New England. The curious will find these quaint craft entertainingly described by Wallace B. Ordway in "The Merrimac River Gundalow and Gundalowman," *The American Neptune* X (1950), pages 249–263. And see William Hutchinson Rowe, *The Maritime History of Maine* (N.Y. 1950), pages 49–50.

itants with greater advantage and security to themselves than the traveler in a coach, who would be unable to indulge in such broadsides of wit and humor in so small a vessel for fear of the recoil. They are not subject to great exposure, like the lumberers of Maine, in any weather, but inhale the healthfulest breezes, being slightly incumbered with clothing, frequently with the head and feet bare.

When we met them at noon, as they were leisurely descending the stream, their busy commerce did not look like toil, but rather like some ancient Oriental game still played on a large scale, as the game of chess, for instance, handed down to this generation. From morning till night, unless the wind is so fair that his single sail will suffice without other labor than steering, the boatman walks backwards and forwards on the side of his boat, now stooping with his shoulder to the pole, then drawing it back slowly to set it again, meanwhile moving steadily forward through an endless valley and an ever-changing scenery, now distinguishing his course for a mile or two, and now shut in by a sudden turn of the river in a small woodland lake. All the phenomena which surround him are simple and grand, and there is something impressive, even majestic, in the very motion he causes, which will naturally be communicated to his own character, and he feels the slow, irresistible movement under him with pride, as if it were his own energy.

The news spread like wildfire among us youths, when formerly, once in a year or two, one of these boats came up the Concord River, and was seen stealing mysteriously through the meadows and past the village. It came and departed as silently as a cloud, without noise or dust, and was witnessed by few. One summer day this huge traveler might be seen moored at some meadow's wharf, and another summer day it was not there. Where precisely it came from, or who these men were who knew the rocks and soundings better than we who bathed there, we could never tell. We knew some river's bay only, but they took rivers from end to end.

They were a sort of fabulous rivermen to us. It was inconceivable by what sort of mediation any mere landsman could hold communicaion with them. Would they heave to, to gratify his wishes? No, it was favor enough to know faintly of their destination, or the time of their possible return. I have seen them in the summer, when the stream ran low, mowing the weeds in mid-channel, and with hayers' jests cutting broad swaths in three feet of water, that they might make a passage for their scow, while the grass in long windrows was carried down the stream, undried by the rarest hay-weather. We admired unweariedly how their vessel would float, like a huge chip, sustaining so many casks of lime, and thousands of bricks, and such heaps of iron ore, with wheelbarrows aboard, and that, when we stepped on it, it did not yield to the pressure of our feet. It gave us confidence in the prevalence of the law of buoyancy, and we imagined to what infinite uses it might be put.

The men appeared to lead a kind of life on it, and it was whispered that they slept aboard. Some affirmed that it carried sail, and that such winds blew here as filled the sails of vessels on the ocean; which again others much doubted. They had been seen to sail across our Fair Haven bay by lucky fishers who were out, but unfortunately others were not there to see. We might then say that our river was navigable, — why not? In after years I read in print, with no little satisfaction, that it was thought by some that, with a little expense in removing rocks and deepening the channel, "there might be a profitable inland navigation." *I* then lived somewhere to tell of.

Such is Commerce, which shakes the cocoanut and bread-fruit tree in the remotest isle, and sooner or later dawns on the duskiest and most simple-minded savage. If we may be pardoned the digression, who can help being affected at the thought of the very fine and slight, but positive relation, in which the savage inhabitants of some remote isle stand to the mysterious white mariner, the child of the sun? — as if *we* were to have dealings with an animal higher in the scale of being than ourselves. It is a barely recognized fact to the natives that he exists, and has his home far away somewhere, and is glad to buy their fresh fruits with his superfluous commodities. Under the same catholic sun glances his white ship over Pacific waves into their smooth bays, and the poor savage's paddle gleams in the air.

Since our voyage the railroad on the bank has been extended, and there is now but little boating on the Merrimack.[1] All kinds of produce and stores were formerly conveyed by water, but now nothing is carried up the stream, and almost wood and bricks alone are carried down, and these are also carried on the railroad. The locks are fast wearing out, and will soon be impassable, since the tolls will not pay the expense of repairing them, and so in a few years there will be an end of boating on this river. The boating at present is principally between Merrimack and Lowell, or Hooksett and Manchester. They make two or three trips in a week, according to wind and weather, from Merrimack to Lowell and back, about twenty-five miles each way. The boatman comes singing in to shore late at night, and moors his empty boat, and gets his supper and lodging in some house near at hand, and again early in the morning, by starlight perhaps, he pushes

---

[1] The competition of the railroads had commenced even prior to Thoreau's river trip when the Boston and Lowell Railroad, which ran parallel to the Canal, was opened to public travel in the summer of 1835. And albeit, as the text has indicated, there was still construction at Tyngsborough, there had been some traffic on the Lowell and Nashua in 1839. By 1842 the Concord and Nashua Railroad was in operation. This, for all practical purposes, was the end: the Canal was doomed. In 1840 the agent for the Proprietors reported to them that with the full operation of the railroad as far as Nashua, the receipts from tolls had been cut two-thirds. The picturesque river traffic dwindled fast, and the last canal boat passed through the Canal in the fall of 1851. In 1860 the Proprietors lost their charter, and this was the official end of the Middlesex Canal.

away upstream, and, by a shout, or the fragment of a song, gives notice of his approach to the lock-man, with whom he is to take his breakfast. If he gets up to his wood-pile before noon he proceeds to load his boat, with the help of his single "hand," and is on his way down again before night.

When he gets to Lowell he unloads his boat, and gets his receipt for his cargo, and, having heard the news at the public house at Middlesex or elsewhere, goes back with his empty boat and his receipt in his pocket to the owner, and to get a new load. We were frequently advertised of their approach by some faint sound behind us, and looking round saw them a mile off, creeping stealthily up the side of the stream like alligators. It was pleasant to hail these sailors of the Merrimack from time to time, and learn the news which circulated with them. We imagined that the sun shining on their bare heads had stamped a liberal and public character on their most private thoughts.

The open and sunny intervale still stretched away from the river sometimes by two or more terraces, to the distant hill-country, and when we climbed the bank, we commonly found an irregular copse-wood skirting the river, the primitive having floated downstream long ago to —— the "King's navy." Sometimes we saw the river-road a quarter or half a mile distant, and the particolored Concord stage, with its cloud of dust, its van of earnest traveling faces, and its rear of dusty trunks, reminding us that the country had its places of rendezvous for restless Yankee men.

There dwelt along at considerable distances on this intervale a quiet agricultural and pastoral people, with every house its well, as we sometimes proved, and every household, though never so still and remote it appeared in the noontide, its dinner about these times. There they lived on, those New England people, farmer lives, father and grandfather and great-grandfather, on and on without noise, keeping up tradition, and expecting, beside fair weather and abundant harvests, we did not learn what. They were contented to live, since it was so contrived for them, and where their lines had fallen. Yet these men had no need to travel to be as wise as Solomon in all his glory, so similar are the lives of men in all countries, and fraught with the same homely experiences. One half the world *knows* how the other half lives.

About noon we passed a small village in Merrimack at Thornton's Ferry, and tasted of the waters of Naticook Brook on the same side, where French and his companions, whose grave we saw in Dunstable, were ambuscaded by the Indians. The humble village of Litchfield, with its steepleless meeting-house, stood on the opposite or east bank, near where a dense grove of willows backed by maples skirted the shore. There also we noticed some shagbark-trees, which, as they do not grow in Concord, were as strange a sight to us as the palm would be, whose fruit only we have seen. Our course now curved gracefully to the north, leaving a low, flat shore on the Merrimack side, which forms a sort of harbor for canal-boats. We observed some fair elms and particularly large and handsome white-maples standing conspicuously on this intervale; and the opposite shore, a quarter of a mile below, was covered with young elms and maples six inches high, which had probably sprung from the seeds which had been washed across.

Some carpenters were at work here mending a scow on the green and sloping bank. The strokes of their mallets echoed from shore to shore, and up and down the river, and their tools gleamed in the sun a quarter of a mile from us, and we realized that boat-building was as ancient and honorable an art as agriculture, and that there might be a naval as well as a pastoral life. The whole history of commerce was made manifest in that scow turned bottom upward on the shore. Thus did men begin to go down upon the sea in ships; *quœque diu steterant in montibus altis, Fluctibus ignotis insultavere carinœ;* "and keels which had long stood on high mountains careered insultingly (*insultavere*) over unknown waves."[1]

We thought that it would be well for the traveler to build his boat on the bank of a stream, instead of finding a ferry or a bridge. In the Adventures of Henry the fur-trader, it is pleasant to read that when with his Indians he reached the shore of Ontario, they consumed two days

---

[1] Ovid., Met. I 133. [Thoreau.]

HENRY
BUGBEE
KANE

in making two canoes of the bark of the elm-tree, in which to transport themselves to Fort Niagara. It is a worthy incident in a journey, a delay as good as much rapid traveling. A good share of our interest in Xenophon's story of his retreat is in the manœuvres to get the army safely over the rivers, whether on rafts of logs or fagots, or sheep-skins blown up. And where could they better afford to tarry meanwhile than on the banks of a river?

As we glided past at a distance, these outdoor workmen appeared to have added some dignity to their labor by its very publicness. It was a part of the industry of nature, like the work of hornets and mud-wasps. The haze, the sun's dust of travel, had a Lethean influence on the land and its inhabitants, and all creatures resigned themselves to float upon the inappreciable tides of nature.

The routine which is in the sunshine and the finest days, as that which has conquered and prevailed, commends itself to us by its very antiquity and apparent solidity and necessity. Our weakness needs it, and our strength uses it. We cannot draw on our boots without bracing ourselves against it. If there were but one erect and solid-standing tree in the woods, all creatures would go to rub against it and make sure of their footing. During the many hours which we spend in this waking sleep, the hand stands still on the face of the clock, and we grow like corn in the night. Men are as busy as the brooks or bees, and postpone everything to their business; as carpenters discuss politics between the strokes of the hammer while they are shingling a roof.

This noontide was a fit occasion to make some pleasant harbor, and there read the journal of some voyageur like ourselves, not too moral nor inquisitive, and which would not disturb the noon; or else some old classic, the very flower of all reading, which we had postponed to such a season "Of Syrian peace, immortal leisure." But, alas, our chest, like the cabin of a coaster, contained only its well-thumbed "Navigator" for all literature, and we were obliged to draw on our memory for these things.

We naturally remembered Alexander Henry's Adventures here, as a sort of classic among books of American travel. It contains scenery and rough sketching of men and incidents enough to inspire poets for many years, and to my fancy is as full of sounding names as any page of history, — Lake Winnipeg, Hudson's Bay, Ottaway, and portages innumerable; Chippeways, Gens de Terres, Les Pilleurs, The Weepers; with reminiscences of Hearne's journey, and the like; an immense and shaggy but sincere country, summer and winter, adorned with chains of lakes and rivers, covered with snows, with hemlocks, and fir-trees.

There is a naturalness, an unpretending and cold life in this traveler, as in a Canadian winter, what life was preserved through low temperatures and frontier dangers by furs within a stout heart. He has truth and moderation worthy of the father of history, which belong only to an intimate experience, and he does not defer too much to literature. The unlearned traveler may quote his single line from the poets with as good right as the scholar. He too may speak of the stars, for he sees them shoot perhaps when the astronomer does not. The good sense of this author is very conspicuous. He is a traveler who does not exaggerate, but writes for the information of his readers, for science, and for history. His story is told with as much good faith and directness as if it were a report to his brother traders, or the Directors of the Hudson's Bay Company, and is fitly dedicated to Sir Joseph Banks.[1]

It reads like the argument to a great poem on the primitive state of the country and its inhabitants, and the reader imagines what in each case, with the invocation of the Muse, might be sung, and leaves off with suspended interest, as if the full account were to follow. In what school was this fur-trader educated? He seems to travel the immense snowy country with such purpose only as the reader who accompanies him, and to the latter's imagination, it is, as it were, momentarily created to be the scene of his adventures. What is most interesting and valuable in it, however, is not the materials for the history of Pontiac, or Braddock, or the Northwest, which it

[1] *Travels and Adventures in Canada and the Indian Territories,* by Alexander Henry, Esq., New York, 1809. This book comprises the author's experiences in the Canadian wilds and among the Indians as a fur trader upon two extended trips in the sixteen years following the fall of Quebec in 1759. It reads like a diary of Francis Parkman.

furnishes; not the *annals* of the country, but the natural facts, or *perennials,* which are ever without date. When out of history the truth shall be extracted, it will have shed its dates like withered leaves.

The Souhegan, or *Crooked* River, as some translate it, comes in from the west about a mile and a half above Thornton's Ferry. Baboosuck Brook empties into it near its mouth. There are said to be some of the finest water privileges in the country still unimproved on the former stream, at a short distance from the Merrimack. One spring morning, March 22, in the year 1677, an incident occurred on the banks of the river here, which is interesting to us as a slight memorial of an interview between two ancient tribes of men, one of which is now extinct, while the other, though it is still represented by a miserable remnant, has long since disappeared from its ancient hunting-grounds. A Mr. James Parker, at "Mr. Hinchmanne's farme ner Meremack," wrote thus "to the Honred Governer and Council at Bostown, *Hast, Post Hast:*" —

"Sagamore Wanalancet come this morning to informe me, and then went to Mr. Tyng's to informe him, that his son being on ye other sid of Meremack river over against Souhegan upon the 22 day of this instant, about tene of the clock in the morning, he discovered 15 Indians on this sid the river, which he soposed to be Mohokes by ther spech. He called to them; they answered but he could not understand ther spech; and he having a conow ther in the river, he went to breck his conow that they might not have ani ues of it. In the mean time they shot about thirty guns at him, and he being much frighted fled, and come home forthwith to Nahamcock [Pawtucket Falls or Lowell], wher ther wigowames now stand."

Penacooks and Mohawks! *ubique gentium sunt?* In the year 1670, a Mohawk warrior scalped a Naamkeak or else a Wamesit Indian maiden near where Lowell now stands. She, however, recovered. Even as late af 1685, John Hogkins, a Penacook Indian, who describes his grandfather as having lived "at place called Malamake rever, other name chef Natukkog and Panukkog, that one rever great many names," wrote thus to the governor: —

> May 15th, 1685
>
> Honor governor my friend,—
>
> You my friend I desire your worship and your power, because I hope you can do som great matters this one. I am poor and naked and I have no men at my place because I afraid allwayes Mohogs he will kill me every day and night. If your worship when please pray help me you no let Mohogs kill me at my place at Malamake river called Pannukkog and Natukkog, I will submit your worship and your power. And now I want pouder and such alminishon shatt and guns, because I have forth at my hom and I plant theare.
>
> This all Indian hand, but pray you do consider your humble servant,
>
> JOHN HOGKINS

Signed also by Simon Detogkom, King Hary, Sam Linis,

Mr. Jorge Rodunnonukgus, John Owamosimmin, and nine other Indians, with their marks against their names.

But now, one hundred and fifty-four years having elapsed since the date of this letter, we went unalarmed on our way without "brecking" our "conow," reading the New England Gazetteer, and seeing no traces of "Mohogs" on the banks.

The Souhegan, though a rapid river, seemed to-day to have borrowed its character from the noon. During the heat of the day, we rested on a large island a mile above the mouth of this river, pastured by a herd of cattle, with steep banks and scattered elms and oaks, and a sufficient channel for canal-boats on each side. When we made a fire to boil some rice for our dinner, the flames spreading amid the dry grass, and the smoke curling silently upward and casting grotesque shadows on the ground, seemed phenomena of the noon, and we fancied that we progressed up the stream without effort, and as naturally as the wind and tide went down, not outraging the calm days by unworthy bustle or impatience.

The woods on the neighboring shore were alive with pigeons, which were moving south, looking for mast, but now, like ourselves, spending their noon in the shade.[1] We could hear the slight, wiry, winnowing sound of their wings as they changed their roosts from time to time, and their gentle and tremulous cooing. They sojourned with

[1] The word "mast" means "nuts" collectively; and in the case of these pigeons, "acorns."

us during the noontide, greater travelers far than we. You may frequently discover a single pair sitting upon the lower branches of the white-pine in the depths of the wood, at this hour of the day, so silent and solitary, and with such a hermit-like appearance, as if they had never strayed beyond its skirts, while the acorn which was gathered in the forests of Maine is still undigested in their crops.

We obtained one of these handsome birds, which lingered too long upon its perch, and plucked and broiled it here with some other game, to be carried along for our supper; for, beside the provisions which we carried with us, we depended mainly on the river and forest for our supply. It is true, it did not seem to be putting this bird to its right use to pluck off its feathers, and extract its entrails, and broil its carcass on the coals; but we heroically persevered, nevertheless, waiting for further information.[1]

---

[1] This was the famed and now extinct passenger pigeon (*Ectopistes migratorius*) the flights of whose flocks once darkened the sky. Thoreau

The same regard for Nature which excited our sympathy for her creatures nerved our hands to carry through what we had begun. For we would be honorable to the

---

was entranced with these lovely creatures, and his journals reflect more than two score entries about them. On September 12, 1851, he wrote:

"Saw a pigeon-place on George Heywood's cleared lot, — the six dead trees set up for the pigeons to alight on, and the brush house close by to conceal the man. I was rather startled to find such a thing going now in Concord. The pigeons on the trees looked like fabulous birds with their long tails and their pointed breasts. I could hardly believe they were alive and not some wooden birds used for decoys, they sat so still; and, even when they moved their necks, I thought it was the effect of art. As they were not catching then, I approached and scared away a dozen birds who were perched on the trees, and found that they were freshly baited there, though the net was carried away, perchance to some other bed. The smooth sandy bed was covered with buckwheat, wheat or rye, and acorns. Sometimes they use corn, shaved off the ear in its present state with a knife. There were left the sticks with which they fastened the nets. As I stood there, I heard a rushing sound and, looking up, saw a flock of thirty or forty pigeons dashing toward the *trees,* who suddenly whirled on seeing me and circled round and made a new dash toward the bed, as if they would fain alight if I had not been there, then steered off. I crawled into the bough house and lay awhile looking through the leaves, hoping to see them come again and feed, but they did not while I stayed. This net and bed belong to one Harrington of Weston, as I hear. Several men still take pigeons in Concord every year; by a method, methinks, extremely old and which I seem to have seen pictured in some old book of fables or symbols, and yet few in Concord know exactly how it is done. And yet it is all done for money and because the birds fetch a good price, just as the farmers raise corn and potatoes. I am always expecting that those engaged in such a pursuit will be somewhat less grovelling and mercenary than the regular trader or farmer, but I fear that it is not so."

Eight years later almost to a day he recorded:

"I sat near Coombs's pigeon-place by White Pond. The pigeons sat motionless on his bare perches, from time to time dropping down into the bed and uttering a *quivet* or two. Some stood on the perch; others squatted flat. I could see their dove-colored breasts. Then all at once, being alarmed, would take flight, but ere long return in straggling parties. He tells me that he has fifteen dozen baited, but does not intend to catch any more at present, or for two or three weeks, hoping to attract others. Rice says that white oak acorns pounded up, shells and all, make the best bait for them."

party we deserted; we would fulfill fate, and so at length, perhaps, detect the secret innocence of these incessant tragedies which Heaven allows. We are doubled-edged blades, and every time we whet our virtue the return stroke straps our vice. Where is the skillful swordsman who can give clean wounds, and not rip up his work with the other edge?

Nature herself has not provided the most graceful end for her creatures. What becomes of all these birds that people the air and forest for our solacement? The sparrows seem always *chipper*, never infirm. We do not see their bodies lie about. Yet there is a tragedy at the end of each one of their lives. They must perish miserably; not one of them is translated. True, "not a sparrow falleth to the ground without our Heavenly Father's knowledge," but they do fall, nevertheless.

The carcasses of some poor squirrels, however, the same that frisked so merrily in the morning, which we had skinned and emboweled for our dinner, we abandoned in disgust, with tardy humanity, as too wretched a resource for any but starving men. It was to perpetuate the practice of a barbarous era. If they had been larger, our crime had been less. Their small red bodies, little bundles of red tissue, mere gobbets of venison, would not have "fattened fire." With a sudden impulse we threw them away, and washed our hands, and boiled some rice for our dinner.

"Behold the difference between the one who eateth flesh, and him to whom it belonged! The first hath a momentary enjoyment, whilst the latter is deprived of existence!" "Who would commit so great a crime against a poor animal, who is fed only by the herbs which grow wild in the woods, and whose belly is burnt up with hunger?" We remembered a picture of mankind in the hunter age, chasing hares down the mountains; O me miserable! Yet sheep and oxen are but larger squirrels, whose hides are saved and meat is salted, whose souls perchance are not so large in proportion to their bodies.

There should always be some flowering and maturing of the fruits of nature in the cooking process. Some simple dishes recommend themselves to our imaginations as well as palates. In parched corn, for instance, there is a manifest sympathy between the bursting seed and the more perfect developments of vegetable life. It is a perfect flower with its petals, like the houstonia or anemone. On my warm hearth these cerealian blossoms expanded; here is the bank whereon they grew. Perhaps some such visible blessing would always attend the simple and wholesome repast.

Here was that "pleasant harbor" which we had sighed for, where the weary voyageur could read the journal of some other sailor, whose bark had ploughed, perchance, more famous and classic seas. At the tables of the gods, after feasting follow music and song; we will recline now under these island trees, and for our minstrel call on Anacreon.[1]

Late in the afternoon, for we had lingered long on the island, we raised our sail for the first time, and for a short hour the southwest wind was our ally; but it did not please Heaven to abet us long. With one sail raised we swept slowly up the eastern side of the stream, steering clear of the rocks, while, from the top of a hill which formed the opposite bank, some lumberers were rolling down timber to be rafted down the stream. We could see their axes and levers gleaming in the sun, and the logs came down with a dust and a rumbling sound, which was reverberated through the woods beyond us on our side, like the roar of artillery.[2] But Zephyr soon took us out of sight and hearing of this commerce.

Having passed Read's Ferry, and another island called McGaw's Island, we reached some rapids called Moore's Falls, and entered on "that section of the river, nine miles in extent, converted, by law, into the Union Canal, comprehending in that space six distinct falls; at each of

---

[1] There then follows a discussion of the classics and some translations of Anacreon.

[2] The phrase "log-rolling," which survives in the slang of our politics, took its rise from such a scene as this. Thoreau's acount of his excursion up the West Branch of the Penobscot to make the ascent of Mount Ktaadn in September 1846 is replete with passages descriptive of lumbering operations and river driving. This had appeared (in the year before the publication of *A Week on the Concord and Merrimac Rivers*) in the *Union Magazine* (New York), and was later incorporated in *The Maine Woods* (1864).

which, and at several intermediate places, work has been done." After passing Moore's Falls by means of locks, we again had recourse to our oars, and went merrily on our way, driving the small sandpiper from rock to rock before us, and sometimes rowing near enough to a cottage on the bank, though they were few and far between, to see the sunflowers, and the seed vessels of the poppy, like small goblets filled with the water of Lethe, before the door, but without disturbing the sluggish household behind.

Thus we held on, sailing or dipping our way along with the paddle up this broad river, smooth and placid, flowing over concealed rocks, where we could see the pickerel lying low in the transparent water, eager to double some distant cape, to make some great bend as in the life of man, and see what new perspective would open; looking far into a new country, broad and serene, the cottages of settlers seen afar for the first time, yet with the moss of a century on their roofs, and the third or fourth generation in their shadows. Strange was it to consider how the sun and the summer, the buds of spring and the seared leaves of autumn, were related to these cabins along the shore; how all the rays which paint the landscape radiate from them, and the flight of the crow and the gyrations of the hawk have reference to their roofs. Still the ever rich and fertile shores accompanied us, fringed with vines and alive with small birds and frisking squirrels, the edge of some farmer's field or widow's wood-lot, or wilder, perchance, where the muskrat, the little medicine of the river, drags itself along stealthily over the alder-leaves and muscle-shells, and man and the memory of man are banished far.

At length the unwearied, never-sinking shore, still holding on without break, with its cool copses and serene pasture-grounds, tempted us to disembark; and we adventurously landed on this remote coast, to survey it, without the knowledge of any human inhabitant probably to this day. But we still remember the gnarled and hospitable oaks which grew even there for our entertainment, and were no strangers to us, the lonely horse in his pasture, and the patient cows, whose path to the river, so judiciously chosen to overcome the difficulties of the way, we followed, and disturbed their ruminations in the shade; and, above all, the cool, free aspect of the wild apple-trees, generously proffering their fruit to us, though still green and crude, — the hard, round, glossy fruit, which, if not ripe, still was not poison, but New English too, brought hither its ancestors by ours once. These gentler trees imparted a half-civilized and twilight aspect to the otherwise barbarian land.

Still farther on we scrambled up the rocky channel of a brook, which had long served nature for a sluice there, leaping like it from rock to rock, through tangled woods, at the bottom of a ravine, which grew darker and darker, and more and more hoarse the murmurs of the stream, until we reached the ruins of a mill, where now the ivy grew, and the trout glanced through the crumbling flume; and there we imagined what had been the dreams and speculations of some early settler. But the waning day compelled us to embark once more, and redeem this wasted time with long and vigorous sweeps over the rippling stream.

It was still wild and solitary, except that at intervals of a mile or two the roof of a cottage might be seen over the bank. This region, as we read, was once famous for the manufacture of straw bonnets of the Leghorn kind, of which it claims the invention in these parts; and occasionally some industrious damsel tripped down to the water's edge, to put her straw a-soak, as it appeared, and stood awhile to watch the retreating voyageurs, and catch the fragments of a boat-song which we had made, wafted over the water.

Just before sundown we reached some more falls in the town of Bedford, where some stonemasons were employed repairing the locks in a solitary part of the river. They were interested in our adventure, especially one young man of our own age, who inquired at first if we were bound up to " 'Skeag;" and when he had heard our story, and examined our outfit, asked us other questions, but temperately still, and always turning to his work again, though as if it were become his duty. It was plain that he would like to go with us, and, as he looked up the river, many a distant cape and wooded shore were reflected in his eye, as well as in his thoughts. When we were ready he left his work, and helped us through the locks with a sort of quiet enthusiasm, telling us that we were at Coos Falls, and we could still distinguish the strokes of his chisel for many sweeps after we had left him.

We wished to camp this night on a large rock in the middle of the stream, just above these falls, but the want of fuel, and the difficulty of fixing our tent firmly, prevented us; so we made our bed on the main-land opposite, on the west bank, in the town of Bedford, in a retired place, as we supposed, there being no house in sight.

6. Wednesday

Early this morning, as we were rolling up our buffaloes and loading our boat amid the dew, while our embers were still smoking, the masons who worked at the locks, and whom we had seen crossing the river in their boat the evening before while we were examining the rock, came upon us as they were going to their work, and we found that we had pitched our tent directly in the path to their boat. This was the only time that we were observed on our camping-ground. Thus, far from the beaten highways and the dust and din of travel, we beheld the country privately, yet freely, and at our leisure. Other roads do some violence to Nature, and bring the traveler to stare at her, but the river steals into the scenery it traverses without intrusion, silently creating and adorning it, and is as free to come and go as the zephyr.

As we shoved away from this rocky coast, before sunrise, the smaller bittern, the genius of the shore, was moping along its edge, or stood probing the mud for its food, with ever an eye on us, though so demurely at work, or else he ran along over the wet stones like a wrecker in his storm coat, looking out for wrecks of snails and cockles. Now away he goes, with a limping flight, uncertain where he will alight, until a rod of clear sand amid the alders invites his feet; and now our steady approach compels him to seek a new retreat. It is a bird of the oldest Thalesian school, and no doubt believes in the priority of water to the other elements; the relic of a twilight antediluvian age which yet inhabits these bright American rivers with us Yankees.[1]

There is something venerable in this melancholy and contemplative race of birds, which may have trodden the earth while it was yet in a slimy and imperfect state. Perchance their tracks, too, are still visible on the stones. It still lingers into our glaring summers, bravely supporting its fate without sympathy from man, as if it looked forward to some second advent of which *he* has no assurance. One wonders if, by its patient study by

[1] *Ixobrychus exilis* (the least bittern).

rocks and sandy capes, it has wrested the whole of her secret from Nature yet. What a rich experience it must have gained, standing on one leg and looking out from its dull eye so long on sunshine and rain, moon and stars! What could it tell of stagnant pools and reeds and dank night-fogs! It would be worth the while to look closely into the eye which has been open and seeing at such hours, and in such solitudes, its dull, yellowish, greenish eye. Methinks my own soul must be a bright invisible green. I have seen these birds stand by the half dozen together in the shallower water along the shore, with their bills thrust into the mud at the bottom, probing for food, the whole head being concealed, while the neck and body formed an arch above the water.

Cohass Brook, the outlet of Massabesic Pond, — which last is five or six miles distant, and contains fifteen hundred acres, being the largest body of fresh water in Rockingham County, — comes in near here from the east. Rowing between Manchester and Bedford, we passed, at an early hour, a ferry and some falls, called Goff's Falls, the Indian Cohasset, where there is a small village, and a handsome green islet in the middle of the stream. From Bedford and Merrimack have been boated the bricks of which Lowell is made.

About twenty years before, as they told us, one Moore, of Bedford, having clay on his farm, contracted to furnish eight millions of bricks to the founders of that city within two years. He fulfilled his contract in one year, and since then bricks have been the principal export from these towns. The farmers found thus a market for their wood, and when they had brought a load to the kilns, they could cart a load of bricks to the shore, and so make a profitable day's work of it. Thus all parties were benefited. It was worth the while to see the place where Lowell was "dug out." So, likewise, Manchester is being built of bricks made still higher up the river at Hooksett.

There might be seen here on the bank of the Merrimack, near Goff's Falls, in what is now the town of Bedford, famous "for hops and for its fine domestic manufactures," some graves of the aborigines. The land still bears this scar here, and time is slowly crumbling the bones of a race. Yet, without fail, every spring, since they first fished and hunted here, the brown thrasher has heralded the morning from a birch or alder spray, and the undying race of reedbirds still rustles through the withering grass. But these bones rustle not. These mouldering elements are slowly preparing for another metamorphosis, to serve new masters, and what was the Indian's will erelong be the white man's sinew.

We learned that Bedford was not so famous for hops as formerly, since the price is fluctuating, and poles are now scarce. Yet if the traveler goes back a few miles from the river, the hop kilns will still excite his curiosity.

There were few incidents in our voyage this forenoon, though the river was now more rocky and the falls more frequent than before. It was a pleasant change, after rowing incessantly for many hours, to lock ourselves through in some retired place, — for commonly there was no lock-man at hand, — one sitting in the boat, while the other, sometimes with no little labor and heave-yo-ing, opened and shut the gates, waiting patiently to see the locks fill. We did not once use the wheels which we had provided. Taking advantage of the eddy, we were sometimes floated up to the locks almost in the face of the falls; and, by the same cause, any floating timber was carried round in a circle and repeatedly drawn into the rapids before it finally went down the stream.[1] These old

---

[1] The vagaries of a stream had a fascination for Thoreau. Two decades later, when descending the East Branch of the Penobscot River, he wrote; describing one of the many pitches:

"After this rough walking in the dark woods it was an agreeable change to glide down the rapid river in the canoe once more. This river, which was about the size of our Assabet (in Concord), though still very swift, was almost perfectly smooth here, and showed a very visible declivity, a regularly inclined plane, for several miles, like a mirror set a little aslant, on which we coasted down. This very obvious regular descent, particularly plain when I regarded the water-line against the shores, made a singular impression on me, which the swiftness of our motion probably enhanced, so that we seemed to be gliding down a much steeper declivity than we were, and that we could not save ourselves from rapids and falls if we should suddenly come upon them. My companion did not perceive this slope, but I have a surveyor's eyes, and

gray structures, with their quiet arms stretched over the river in the sun, appeared like natural objects in the scenery, and the kingfisher and sandpiper alighted on them as readily as on stakes or rocks.

We rowed leisurely up the stream for several hours, until the sun had got high in the sky, our thoughts monotonously beating time to our oars. For outward variety there was only the river and the receding shores, a vista continually opening behind and closing before us, as we sat with our backs upstream; and, for inward, such thoughts as the muses grudgingly lent us. We were always passing some low, inviting shore, or some overhanging bank, on which, however, we never landed.

It might be seen by what tenure men held the earth. The smallest stream is *mediterranean* sea, a smaller ocean creek within the land, where men may steer by their farm bounds and cottage lights. For my own part, but for the geographers, I should hardly have known how large a portion of our globe is water, my life has chiefly passed within so deep a cove. Yet I have sometimes ven-

---

I satisfied myself that it was no ocular illusion."

And on his first trip up the West Branch to climb Mount Ktaadn in 1846, he quoted John S. Springer's *Forest Life and Forest Trees* (N.Y. 1851) page 164, in a footnote where describing a river drive:

"A steady current or pitch of water is preferable to one either rising or diminishing; as, when rising rapidly, the water at the middle of the river is considerably higher than at the shores, — so much so as to be distinctly perceived by the eye of a spectator on the banks, presenting an appearance like a turnpike road. The lumber, therefore, is always sure to incline from the centre of the channel toward either shore."

tured as far as to the mouth of my Snug Harbor. From an old ruined fort on Staten Island, I have loved to watch all day some vessel whose name I had read in the morning through the telegraph glass, when she first came upon the coast, and her hull heaved up and glistened in the sun, from the moment when the pilot and most adventurous news-boat met her, past the Hook, and up the narrow channel of the wide bay, till she was boarded by the health officer, and took her station at Quarantine, or held on her unquestioned course to the wharves of New York.

It was interesting, too, to watch the less adventurous newsman, who made his assault as the vessel swept through the Narrows, defying plague and quarantine law, and, fastening his little cockboat to her huge side, clambered up and disappeared in the cabin. And then I could imagine what momentous news was being imparted by the captain, which no American ear had ever heard, that Asia, Africa, Europe — were all sunk; for which at length he pays the price, and is seen descending the ship's side with his bundle of newspapers, but not where he first got up, for these arrivers do not stand still to gossip; and he hastes away with steady sweeps to dispose of his wares to the highest bidder, and we shall erelong read something startling, — "By the latest arrival," — "by the good ship ——."

On Sunday I beheld, from some interior hill, the long procession of vessels getting to sea, reaching from the city wharves through the Narrows, and past the Hook, quite to the ocean stream, far as the eye could reach, with stately march and silken sails, all counting on lucky voyages, but each time some of the number, no doubt, destined to go to Davy's locker, and never come on this coast again. And, again, in the evening of a pleasant day, it was my amusement to count the sails in sight. But as the setting sun continually brought more and more to light, still farther in the horizon, the last count always had the advantage, till, by the time the last rays streamed over the sea, I had doubled and trebled my first number; though I could no longer class them all under the several heads of ships, barks, brigs, schooners, and sloops, but most were faint generic *vessels* only. And then the temperate twilight light, perchance, revealed the floating home of some sailor whose thoughts were already alienated from this American coast, and directed towards the Europe of our dreams.

I have stood upon the same hill-top, when a thunder-shower, rolling down from the Catskills and Highlands, passed over the island, deluging the land; and, when it had suddenly left us in sunshine, have seen it overtake successively, with its huge shadow and dark descending wall of rain, the vessels in the bay. Their bright sails were suddenly drooping and dark, like the sides of barns, and they seemed to shrink before the storm; while still far beyond them on the sea, through this dark veil, gleamed the sunny sails of those vessels which the storm had not yet reached.

And at midnight, when all around and overhead was darkness, I have seen a field of trembling, silvery light far out on the sea, the reflection of the moonlight from the ocean, as if beyond the precincts of our night, where the moon traversed a cloudless heaven, — and sometimes a dark speck in its midst, where some fortunate vessel was pursuing its happy voyage by night.

But to us river sailors the sun never rose out of ocean waves, but from some green coppice, and went down behind some dark mountain line. We, too, were but dwellers on the shore, like the bittern of the morning; and our pursuit, the wrecks of snails and cockles. Nevertheless, we were contented to know the better one fair particular shore.

The small houses which were scattered along the river at intervals of a mile or more were commonly out of sight to us, but sometimes, when we rowed near the shore, we heard the peevish note of a hen, or some slight domestic sound, which betrayed them. The lock-men's houses were particularly well placed, retired, and high, always at falls or rapids, and commanding the pleasantest reaches of the river, — for it is generally wider and more lake-like just above a fall, — and there they wait for boats. These humble dwellings, homely and sincere, in which a hearth was still the essential part, were more pleasing to our eyes than palaces or castles would have been.

In the noon of these days, as we have said, we occasionally climbed the banks and approached these houses, to get a glass of water and make acquaintance with their inhabitants. High in the leafy bank, surrounded commonly by a small patch of corn and beans, squashes and melons, with sometimes a graceful hop-yard on one side, and some running vine over the windows, they appeared like beehives set to gather honey for a summer. I have not read of any Arcadian life which surpasses the actual luxury and serenity of these New England dwellings. For the outward gilding, at least, the age is golden enough. As you approach the sunny doorway, awakening the echoes by your steps, still no sound from these barracks of repose, and you fear that the gentlest knock may seem rude to the Oriental dreamers.

The door is opened, perchance, by some Yankee-Hindoo woman, whose small-voiced but sincere hospitality, out of the bottomless depths of a quiet nature, has traveled quite round to the opposite side, and fears only to obtrude its kindness. You step over the white-scoured floor to the bright "dresser" lightly, as if afraid to disturb the devotions of the household, — for Oriental dynasties appear to have passed away since the dinner-table was last spread here, — and thence to the frequented curb, where you see your long-forgotten, unshaven face at the bottom, in juxtaposition with new-made butter and the trout in the well. "Perhaps you would like some molasses and ginger," suggests the faint noon voice.

Sometimes there sits the brother who follows the sea,

their representative man; who knows only how far it is to the nearest port, no more distances, all the rest is sea and distant capes, — patting the dog, or dandling the kitten in arms that were stretched by the cable and the oar, pulling against Boreas or the trade-winds. He looks up at the stranger, half pleased, half astonished, with a mariner's eye, as if he were a dolphin within cast. If men will believe it, *sua si bona nôrint,* there are no more quiet Tempes, nor more poetic and Arcadian lives, than may be lived in these New England dwellings. We thought that the employment of their inhabitants by day would be to tend the flowers and herds, and at night, like the shepherds of old, to cluster and give names to the stars from the river banks.

We passed a large and densely wooded island this forenoon, between Short's and Griffith's Falls, the fairest which we had met with, with a handsome grove of elms at its head.[1] If it had been evening, we should have been glad to camp there. Not long after, one or two more were

---

[1] If, while passing through the township of Bedford, the curious sojourner will stop his car just north of Bowman Brook, he may then walk quickly across a field to the shore of the Merrimack. Downstream through the alders is the head of the "large and densely wooded island" — Carthagena, so-called — still "with a handsome grove of elms at its head." Out in the stream in front of one is a series of what the canoeman calls "rips." These are Thoreau's Griffith's Falls. But opposite on the east bank is what you came down to see. There, lining the shore, is a solid wall of granite blocks, rough hewn and massive and draped in the early fall of the year with the scarlet and orange leaves of poison ivy. In front of this wall and between it and a ledge in the river is a narrow passage. These are the remains of the locks, through which they passed on upstream by-passing Griffith's Falls.

passed. The boatmen told us that the current had recently made important changes here.

An island always pleases my imagination, even the smallest, as a small continent and integral portion of the globe. I have a fancy for building my hut on one. Even a bare, grassy isle, which I can see entirely over at a glance, has some undefined and mysterious charm for me. There is commonly such a one at the junction of two rivers, whose currents bring down and deposit their respective sands in the eddy at their confluence, as it were the womb of a continent. By what a delicate and far-stretched contribution every island is made! What an enterprise of Nature thus to lay the foundations of and to build up the future continent, of golden and silver sands and the ruins of forests, with ant-like industry.

Not long after this we saw the Piscataquoag, or Sparkling Water, emptying in on our left, and heard the Falls of Amoskeag above. Large quantities of lumber, as we read in the Gazetteer, were still annually floated down the Piscataquoag to the Merrimack, and there are many fine mill privileges on it. Just above the mouth of this river we passed the artificial falls where the canals of the Manchester Manufacturing Company discharge themselves into the Merrimack. They are striking enough to have a name, and, with the scenery of a Bashpish, would be visited from far and near. The water falls thirty or forty feet over seven or eight steep and narrow terraces of stone, probably to break its force, and is converted into one mass of foam. This canal water did not seem to be the worse for the wear, but foamed and fumed as purely, and boomed as savagely and impressively, as a mountain torrent, and, though it came from under a factory, we saw a rainbow here. These are now the Amoskeag Falls, removed a mile downstream.

But we did not tarry to examine them minutely, making haste to get past the village here collected, and out of hearing of the hammer which was laying the foundation of another Lowell on the banks. At the time of our voyage Manchester was a village of about two thousand inhabitants, where we landed for a moment to get some cool water, and where an inhabitant told us that he was accustomed to go across the river into Goffstown for his water. But now, as I have been told, and indeed have witnessed, it contains fourteen thousand inhabitants.[1] From a hill on the road between Goffstown and Hooksett, four miles distant, I have seen a thunder-shower pass over, and the sun break out and shine on a city there, where I had landed nine years before in the fields; and there was waving the flag of its Museum, where "the only perfect skeleton of a Greenland or river whale in the United States" was to be seen, and I also read in its directory of a "Manchester Athenæum and Gallery of the Fine Arts."

According to the Gazetteer, the descent of Amoskeag

[1] The 1950 figures give 82,732 as the population of Manchester and of Nashua — which Thoreau had described when he passed it as a village — 34,669.

Falls, which are the most considerable in the Merrimack, is fifty-four feet in half a mile. We locked ourselves through here with much ado, surmounting the successive watery steps of this river's staircase in the midst of a crowd of villagers, jumping into the canal to their amusement, to save our boat from upsetting, and consuming

much river water in our service. Amoskeag, or Namaskeak, is said to mean "great fishing-place." It was hereabouts that the Sachem Wannalancet resided.

Tradition says that his tribe, when at war with the Mohawks, concealed their provisions in the cavities of the rocks in the upper part of these falls. The Indians, who hid their provisions in these holes, and affirmed "that God had cut them out for that purpose," understood their origin and use better than the Royal Society, who in their Transactions, in the last century, speaking of these very holes, declare that "they seem plainly to be artificial." Similar "potholes" may be seen at the Stone Flume on this river, on the Ottaway, at Bellows Falls on the Connecticut, and in the limestone rock at Shelburne Falls on

Deerfield River in Massachusetts, and more or less generally about all falls. Perhaps the most remarkable curiosity of this kind in New England is the well-known Basin on the Pemigewasset, one of the head-waters of this river, twenty by thirty feet in extent and proportionably deep, with a smooth and rounded brim, and filled with a cold, pellucid, and greenish water.

At Amoskeag the river is divided into many separate torrents and trickling rills by the rocks, and its volume is so much reduced by the drain of the canals that it does not fill its bed. There are many pot-holes here on a rocky island which the river washes over in high freshets. As at Shelburne Falls, where I first observed them, they are from one foot to four or five in diameter, and as many in depth, perfectly round and regular, with smooth and gracefully curved brims, like goblets.

Their origin is apparent to the most careless observer. A stone which the current has washed down, meeting with obstacles, revolves as a pivot where it lies, gradually sinking in the course of centuries deeper and deeper into the rock, and in new freshets receiving the aid of fresh stones, which are drawn into this trap and doomed to revolve there for an indefinite period, doing Sisyphus-like penance for stony sins, until they either wear out, or wear through the bottom of their prison, or else are released by some revolution of nature. There lie the stones of various sizes, from a pebble to a foot or two in diameter, some of which have rested from their labor only since the spring, and some higher up which have lain still and dry for ages, — we noticed some here at least sixteen feet above the present level of the water, — while others are still revolving, and enjoy no respite at any season.

In one instance, at Shelburne Falls, they have worn quite through the rock, so that a portion of the river leaks through in anticipation of the fall. Some of these pot-holes at Amoskeag, in a very hard brown-stone, had an oblong, cylindrical stone of the same material loosely fitting them. One, as much as fifteen feet deep and seven or eight in diameter, which was worn quite through to the water, had a huge rock of the same material, smooth but of irregular form, lodged in it. Everywhere there were the rudiments or the wrecks of a dimple in the rock; the rocky shells of whirlpools. As if by force of example and sympathy after so many lessons, the rocks, the hardest material, had been endeavoring to whirl or flow into the forms of the most fluid. The finest workers in stone are not copper or steel tools, but the gentle touches of air and water working at their leisure with a liberal allowance of time.

Not only have some of these basins been forming for countless ages, but others exist which must have been completed in a former geological period. In deepening the Pawtucket Canal in 1822, the workmen came to ledges with pot-holes in them, where probably was once the bed of the river, and there are some, we are told, in the town of Canaan in this State, with the stones still in them, on the height of land between the Merrimack and Connecticut, and nearly a thousand feet above these rivers, proving that the mountains and the rivers have changed places. There lie the stones which completed their revolutions perhaps before thoughts began to revolve in the brain of man.

The periods of Hindoo and Chinese history, though they reach back to the time when the race of mortals is confounded with the race of gods, are as nothing compared with the periods which these stones have inscribed. That which commenced a rock when time was young shall conclude a pebble in the unequal contest. With such expense of time and natural forces are our very pavingstones produced. They teach us lessons, these dumb workers; verily there are "sermons in stones, and books in the running brooks." In these very holes the Indians hid their provisions; but now there is no bread, but only its old neighbor stones at the bottom. Who knows how many races they have served thus? By as simple a law, some accidental bylaw, perchance, our system itself was made ready for its inhabitants.

These, and such as these, must be our antiquities, for lack of human vestiges. The monuments of heroes and the temples of the gods which may once have stood on the banks of this river are now, at any rate, returned to dust and primitive soil. The murmur of unchronicled nations has died away along these shores, and once more Lowell and Manchester are on the trail of the Indian.

In these parts dwelt the famous Sachem Pasaconaway, who was seen by Gookin "at Pawtucket, when he was about one hundred and twenty years old." He was reputed a wise man and a powwow, and restrained his people from going to war with the English. They believed "that he could make water burn, rocks move, and trees dance, and metamorphose himself into a flaming man; that in winter he could raise a green leaf out of the ashes of a dry one, and produce a living snake from the skin of a dead one, and many similar miracles."

In 1660, according to Gookin, at a great feast and dance, he made his farewell speech to his people, in which he said that as he was not likely to see them met together again, he would leave them this word of advice, to take heed how they quarreled with their English neighbors, for though they might do them much mischief at first, it would prove the means of their own destruction. He himself, he said, had been as much an enemy to the English at their first coming as any, and had used all his arts to destroy them, or at least to prevent their settlement, but could by no means effect it.

Gookin thought that he "possibly might have such a kind of spirit upon him as was upon Balaam, who, in Numbers xxiii. 23, said, 'Surely, there is no enchantment against Jacob, neither is there any divination against Israel.' " His son Wannalancet carefully followed his advice, and when Philip's war broke out, he withdrew his followers to Penacook, now Concord in New Hampshire, from the scene of the war. On his return afterwards, he visited the minister of Chelmsford, and, as is stated in the history of that town, "wished to know whether Chelmsford had suffered much during the war; and being informed that it had not, and that God should be thanked for it, Wannalancet replied, 'Me next.' "

Manchester was the residence of John Stark, a hero of two wars, and survivor of a third, and at his death the last but one of the American generals of the Revolution. He was born in the adjoining town of Londonderry, then Nutfield, in 1728. As early as 1752, he was taken prisoner by the Indians while hunting in the wilderness near Baker's River; he performed notable service as a captain of rangers in the French war; commanded a regiment of the New Hampshire militia at the battle of Bunker Hill; and fought and won the battle of Bennington in 1777. He was past service in the last war, and died here in 1822, at the age of ninety-four.

His monument stands upon the second bank of the river, about a mile and a half above the falls, and commands a prospect several miles up and down the Merrimack. It suggested how much more impressive in the landscape is the tomb of a hero than the dwellings of the inglorious living. Who is most dead, — a hero by whose monument you stand, or his descendants of whom you have never heard? The graves of Pasaconaway and Wannalancet are marked by no monument on the bank of their native river.

Every town which we passed, if we may believe the Gazetteer, had been the residence of some great man. But though we knocked at many doors, and even made particular inquiries, we could not find that there were any now living. Under the head of Litchfield we read: —

"The Hon. Wyseman Clagett closed his life in this town." According to another, "He was a classical scholar, a good lawyer, a wit, and a poet." We saw his old gray house just below Great Nesenkeag Brook. — Under the head of Merrimack: "Hon. Matthew Thornton, one of the signers of the Declaration of American Independence, resided many years in this town." His house too we saw from the river.

"Dr. Jonathan Gove, a man distinguished for his urbanity, his talents and professional skill, resided in this town [Goffstown]. He was one of the oldest practitioners of medicine in the county. He was many years an active member of the legislature." — "Hon. Robert Means, who died January 24, 1823, at the age of 80, was for a long period a resident in Amherst. He was a native of Ireland. In 1764 he came to this country, where, by his industry and application to business, he acquired a large property, and great respect."

"William Stinson [one of the first settlers of Dunbarton], born in Ireland, came to Londonderry with his father. He was much respected and was a useful man. James Rogers was from Ireland, and father to Major Robert Rogers. He was shot in the woods, being mistaken for a bear." —

"Rev. Matthew Clark, second minister of Londenderry, was a native of Ireland, who had in early life been an officer in the army, and distinguished himself in the defense of the city of Londonderry, when beseiged by the army of King James II., A. D. 1688–89. He afterwards relinquished a military life for the clerical profession. He possessed a strong mind, marked by a considerable degree of eccentricity. He died January 25, 1735, and was borne to the grave, at his particular request, by his former companions in arms, of whom there were a considerable number among the early settlers of this town; several of them had been made free from taxes throughout the British dominions by King William, for their bravery in that memorable seige."

Colonel George Reid and Captain David M'Clary, also citizens of Londonderry, were "distinguished and brave" officers. — "Major Andrew M'Clary, a native of this town [Epsom], fell at the battle of Breed's Hill." Many of these heroes, like the illustrious Roman, were ploughing when the news of the massacre at Lexington arrived, and straightway left their ploughs in the furrow, and repaired to the scene of action. Some miles from where we now were, there once stood a guide-post on which were the words, "3 miles to Squire MacGaw's." But generally speaking, the land is now, at any rate, very barren of men, and we doubt if there are as many hundreds as we read of. It may be that we stood too near.

Uncannunuc Mountain in Goffstown was visible from

Amoskeag, five or six miles westward. It is the northeasternmost in the horizon which we see from our native town, but seen from there is too ethereally blue to be the same which the like of us have ever climbed. Its name is said to mean "The Two Breasts," there being two eminences some distance apart. The highest, which is about fourteen hundred feet above the sea, probably affords a more extensive view of the Merrimack valley and the adjacent country than any other hill, though it is somewhat obstructed by woods. Only a few short reaches of the river are visible, but you can trace its course far downstream by the sandy tracts on its banks.

A little south of Uncannunuc, about sixty years ago, as the story goes, an old woman who went out to gather pennyroyal tripped her foot in the bail of a small brass kettle, in the dead grass and bushes. Some say that flints and charcoal and some traces of a camp were also found. This kettle, holding about four quarts, is still preserved and used to dye thread in. It is supposed to have belonged to some old French or Indian hunter, who was killed in one of his hunting or scouting excursions, and so never returned to look after his kettle.

But we were most interested to hear of the pennyroyal; it is soothing to be reminded that wild nature produces anything ready for the use of man. Men know that *something* is good. One says that it is yellow-dock, another that it is bitter-sweet, another that it is slippery-elm bark, burdock, catnip, calamint, elecampane, thoroughwort, or pennyroyal. A man may esteem himself happy when that which is his food is also his medicine. There is no kind of herb, but somebody or other says that it is good. I am very glad to hear it. It reminds me of the first chapter of Genesis. But how should they know that it is good? That is the mystery to me. I am always agreeably disappointed; it is incredible that they should have found it out.

Since all things are good, men fail at last to distinguish which is the bane and which the antidote. There are sure to be two prescriptions diametrically opposite. Stuff a cold and starve a cold are but two ways. They are the two practices both always in full blast. Yet you must take advice of the one school as if there was no other. In respect to religion and the healing art, all nations are still in a state of barbarism. In the most civilized countries the priest is still but a Powwow, and the physician a Great Medicine. Consider the deference which is everywhere paid to a doctor's opinion. Nothing more strikingly betrays the credulity of mankind than medicine. Quackery is a thing universal, and universally successful. In this case it becomes literally true that no imposition is too great for the credulity of men.

Priests and physicians should never look one another in the face. They have no common ground, nor is there any to mediate between them. When the one comes, the other goes. They could not come together without laughter, or a significant silence, for the one's profession is a satire on the other's, and either's success would be the other's failure. It is wonderful that the physician should ever die, and that the priest should ever live. Why is it that the priest is never called to consult with the physician? Is it because men believe practically that matter is independent of spirit? But what is quackery? It is commonly an attempt to cure the diseases of a man by addressing his body alone. There is need of a physician who shall minister to both soul and body at once, that is, to man. Now he falls between two stools.

After passing through the locks, we had poled ourselves through the canal here, about half a mile in length, to the boatable part of the river. Above Amoskeag the river spreads out into a lake reaching a mile or two without a bend. There were many canal-boats here bound up to Hooksett, about eight miles, and as they were going up empty, with a fair wind, one boatman offered to take us in tow if we would wait. But when we came alongside, we found that they meant to take us on board, since otherwise we should clog their motions too much; but as our boat was too heavy to be lifted aboard, we pursued our way up the stream, as before, while the boatmen were at their dinner, and came to anchor at length under some alders on the oppposite shore, where we could take our lunch.

Though far on one side, every sound was wafted over to us from the opposite bank, and from the harbor of the canal, and we could see everything that passed. By and

HENRY
BUGBEE
KANE

by came several canal-boats, at intervals of a quarter of a mile, standing up to Hooksett with a light breeze, and one by one disappeared round a point above. With their broad sails set, they moved slowly up the stream in the sluggish and fitful breeze, like one-winged antediluvian birds, and as if impelled by some mysterious counter-current. It was a grand motion, so slow and stately, this "standing out," as the phrase is, expressing the gradual and steady progress of a vessel, as if it were by mere rectitude and disposition, without shuffling. Their sails, which stood so still, were like chips cast into the current of the air to show which way it set.

At length the boat which we had spoken came along, keeping the middle of the stream, and when within speaking distance, the steersman called out ironically to say that if we could come alongside now, he would take us in tow; but not heeding his taunt, we still loitered in the shade till we had finished our lunch, and when the last boat had disappeared round the point with flapping sail, for the breeze had now sunk to a zephyr, with our own sails set, and plying our oars, we shot rapidly up the stream in pursuit, and as we glided close alongside, while they were vainly invoking Æolus to their aid, we returned their compliment by proposing, if they would throw us a rope, to "take them in tow," to which these Merrimack sailors had no suitable answer ready. Thus we gradually overtook and passed each boat in succession until we had the river to ourselves again.

Our course this afternoon was between Manchester and Goffstown.

Having rowed five or six miles above Amoskeag before sunset, and reached a pleasant part of the river, one of us landed to look for a farmhouse, where we might replenish our stores, while the other remained cruising about the stream, and exploring the opposite shores to find a suitable harbor for the night. In the mean while the canal-boats began to come round a point in our rear, poling their way along close to the shore, the breeze having quite died away. This time there was no offer of assistance, but one of the boatmen only called out to say, as the truest revenge for having been the losers in the race, that he had seen a wood-duck, which we had scared up, sitting on a tall, white pine, half a mile downstream; and he repeated the assertion several times, and seemed really chagrined at the apparent suspicion with which this information was received. But there sat the summer duck still, undisturbed by us.

By and by the other voyageur returned from his inland expedition, bringing one of the natives with him, a little flaxen-headed boy, with some tradition, or small edition, of Robinson Crusoe in his head, who had been charmed by the account of our adventures, and asked his father's leave to join us. He examined, at first from the top of the bank, our boat and furniture, with sparkling eyes, and wished himself already his own man. He was a lively and interesting boy, and we should have been glad to ship him; but Nathan was still his father's boy, and had not come to years of discretion.

We had got a loaf of home-made bread, and musk and water melons for dessert. For this farmer, a clever and well-disposed man, cultivated a large patch of melons for the Hooksett and Concord markets. He hospitably entertained us the next day, exhibiting his hop-fields and kiln and melon patch, warning us to step over the tight rope which surrounded the latter at a foot from the ground, while he pointed to a little bower at one corner, where it connected with the lock of a gun ranging with the line, and where, as he informed us, he sometimes sat in pleasant nights to defend his premises against thieves. We stepped high over the line, and sympathized with our host's on the whole quite human, if not humane, interest in the success of his experiment. That night especially thieves were to be expected, from rumors in the atmosphere, and the priming was not wet.

He was a Methodist man, who had his dwelling between the river and Uncannunuc Mountain; who there belonged, and stayed at home there and by the encouragement of distant political organizations, and by his own tenacity, held a property in his melons, and continued to plant. We suggested melon seeds of new varieties and fruit of foreign flavor to be added to his stock. We had come away up here among the hills to learn the impartial and unbribable beneficence of Nature. Strawberries and melons grow as well in one man's garden as another's, and the sun lodges as kindly under his hillside, — when we had imagined that she inclined rather to some few earnest and faithful souls whom we know.

We found a convenient harbor for our boat on the opposite or east shore, still in Hooksett, at the mouth of a small brook which emptied into the Merrimack, where it would be out of the way of any passing boat in the night, — for they commonly hug the shore if bound upstream, either to avoid the current, or touch the bottom with their poles, — and where it would be accessible without stepping on the clayey shore. We set one of our largest melons to cool in the still water among the alders at the mouth of this creek, but when our tent was pitched and ready, and we went to get it, it had floated out into the stream, and was nowhere to be seen. So taking the boat in the twilight, we went in pursuit of this property, and at length, after long straining of the eyes, its green disk was discovered far down the river, gently floating seaward with many twigs and leaves from the mountains that evening, and so perfectly balanced that it had not keeled at all, and no water had run in at the tap which had been taken out to hasten its cooling.

As we sat on the bank eating our supper, the clear light of the western sky fell on the eastern trees, and was reflected in the water, and we enjoyed so serene an evening as left nothing to describe. We lay awake a long while listening to the murmurs of the brook, in the angle formed by whose bank with the river our tent was pitched, and there was a sort of man interest in its story, which ceases not in freshet or in drought the livelong summer, and the profounder lapse of the river was quite drowned by its din. But the rill, whose "Silver sands and pebbles sing Eternal ditties with the spring," is silenced by the first frosts of winter, while mightier streams, on whose bottom the sun never shines, clogged with sunken rocks and the ruins of forests, from whose surface comes up no murmur, are strangers to the icy fetters which bind fast a thousand contributory rills.

I dreamed this night of an event which had occurred long before. It was a difference with a Friend, which had not ceased to give me pain, though I had no cause to blame myself. But in my dream ideal justice was at length done me for his suspicions, and I received that compensation which I had never obtained in my waking hours. I was unspeakably soothed and rejoiced, even after I awoke, because in dreams we never deceive ourselves, nor are deceived, and this seemed to have the authority of a final judgment.

We bless and curse ourselves. Some dreams are divine, as well as some waking thoughts. Donne sings of one "Who dreamt devoutlier than most use to pray." Dreams are the touchstones of our characters. We are scarcely less afflicted when we remember some unworthiness in our conduct in a dream, than if it had been actual, and the intensity of our grief, which is our atonement, measures the degree by which this is separated from an actual unworthiness. For in dreams we but act a part which must have been learned and rehearsed in our waking hours, and no doubt could discover some waking consent thereto. If this meanness had not its foundation in us, why are we grieved at it? In dreams we see ourselves naked and acting out our real characters, even more clearly than we see others awake. But an unwavering and commanding virtue would compel even its most fantastic and faintest dreams to respect its ever-wakeful authority; as we are accustomed to say carelessly, we should never have *dreamed* of such a thing. Our truest life is when we are in dreams awake.

7. Thursday

When we awoke this morning, we heard the faint, deliberate, and ominous sound of raindrops on our cotton roof. The rain had pattered all night, and now the whole country wept, the drops falling in the river, and on the alders, and in the pastures, and instead of any bow in the heavens, there was the trill of the hairbird all the morning.[1] The cheery faith of this little bird atoned for the silence of the whole woodland choir beside.

When we first stepped abroad, a flock of sheep, led by their rams, came rushing down a ravine in our rear, with heedless haste and unreserved frisking, as if unobserved by man, from some higher pasture where they had spent the night, to taste the herbage by the river-side; but when their leaders caught sight of our white tent through the

[1] The chipping sparrow (*Spizella passerina*), whose nest is lined with horsehair.

mist, struck with sudden astonishment, with their fore-feet braced, they sustained the rushing torrent in their rear, and the whole flock stood stock-still, endeavoring to solve the mystery in their sheepish brains. At length, concluding that it boded no mischief to them, they spread themselves out quietly over the field.

We learned afterward that we had pitched our tent on the very spot which a few summers before had been occupied by a party of Penobscots.[1] We could see rising before us through the mist a dark conical eminence called Hooksett Pinnacle, a landmark to boatmen, and also Uncannunuc Mountain, broad off on the west side of the river.

This was the limit of our voyage, for a few hours more in the rain would have taken us to the last of the locks, and our boat was too heavy to be dragged around the long and numerous rapids which would occur. On foot, however, we continued up along the bank, feeling our way with a stick through the showery and foggy day, and

[1] This is an interesting instance of the timeless use by the Penobscot Indians of New England's streams as their means of transportation. In his Journal, Thoreau mentions their camping on the Concord River. The late N. C. Wyeth, artist and illustrator, had in his studio a birchbark canoe which he had acquired on the upper reaches of the St. George River in Maine after it had been found abandoned on the bank following the death of a Penobscot in a barroom brawl in Thomaston. As a boy the writer of this note recalls Indian camps in the woods near the Scarborough Marshes in Maine, which are formed by the confluence of five tidal rivers. The Indians came by team, hauling their canoes with them. Even today their lithe forms and leathery countenances are often encountered at the summer resorts on the coast of Maine. They come to peddle baskets and sweet grass, but their means of transportation today — *O tempora, O mores!* — is the modern jalopy.

climbing over the slippery logs in our path with as much pleasure and buoyancy as in brightest sunshine; scenting the fragrance of the pines and the wet clay under our feet, and cheered by the tones of invisible waterfalls; with visions of toadstools, and wandering frogs, and festoons of moss hanging from the spruce-trees, and thrushes flitting silent under the leaves; our road still holding together through that wettest of weather, like faith, while we confidently followed its lead. We managed to keep our thoughts dry, however, and only our clothes were wet. It was altogether a cloudy and drizzling day, with occasional brightenings in the mist, when the trill of the tree-sparrow seemed to be ushering in sunny hours.

"Nothing that naturally happens to man can *hurt* him, earthquakes and thunderstorms not excepted," said a man of genius, who at this time lived a few miles farther on our road. When compelled by a shower to take shelter under a tree, we may improve that opportunity for a more minute inspection of some of Nature's works. I have stood under a tree in the woods half a day at a time, during a heavy rain in the summer, and yet employed myself happily and profitably there prying with microscopic eye into the crevices of the bark or the leaves of the fungi at my feet. "Riches are the attendants of the miser; and the heavens rain plenteously upon the mountains."

I can fancy that it would be a luxury to stand up to one's chin in some retired swamp a whole summer day, scenting the wild honeysuckle and bilberry blows, and lulled by the minstrelsy of gnats and mosquitoes! A day passed in the society of those Greek sages, such as described in the Banquet of Xenophon, would not be comparable with the dry wit of decayed cranberry vines, and the fresh Attic salt of the moss-beds. Say twelve hours of genial and familiar converse with the leopard frog; the sun to rise behind alder and dogwood, and climb buoyantly to his meridian of two hands' breadth, and finally sink to rest behind some bold western hummock. To hear the evening chant of the mosquito from a thousand green chapels, and the bittern begin to boom from some concealed fort like a sunset gun! Surely one may as profitably be soaked in the juices of a swamp for one day as pick his way dry-shod over sand. Cold and damp, — are they not as rich experience as warmth and dryness?

At present, the drops come trickling down the stubble while we lie drenched on a bed of withered wild oats, by the side of a bushy hill, and the gathering in of the clouds, with the last rush and dying breath of the wind, and then the regular dripping of twigs and leaves the country over, enhance the sense of inward comfort and sociableness. The birds draw closer and are more familiar under the thick foliage, seemingly composing new strains upon their roosts against the sunshine. What were the amusements of the drawing-room and the library in comparison, if we had them here?

The Pinnacle is a small wooded hill which rises very abruptly to the height of about two hundred feet, near the shore at Hooksett Falls. As Uncannunuc Mountain is perhaps the best point from which to view the valley of the Merrimack, so this hill affords the best view of the river itself. I have sat upon its summit, a precipitous rock only a few rods long, in fairer weather, when the sun was setting and filling the river valley with a flood of light. You can see up and down the Merrimack several miles each way. The broad and straight river, full of light and life, with its sparkling and foaming falls, the islet which divides the stream, the village of Hooksett on the shore almost directly under your feet, so near that you can converse with its inhabitants or throw a stone into its yards, the woodland lake at its western base, and the mountains in the north and northeast, make a scene of rare beauty and completeness, which the traveler should take pains to behold.

We were hospitably entertained in Concord, New Hampshire, which we persisted in calling *New* Concord, as we had been wont, to distinguish it from our native town, from which we had been told that it was named and in part originally settled. This would have been the proper place to conclude our voyage, uniting Concord with Concord by these meandering rivers, but our boat was moored some miles below its port.

The richness of the intervales at Penacook, now Concord, New Hampshire, had been observed by explorers, and, according to the historian of Haverhill, in the "year

1726, considerable progress was made in the settlement, and a road was cut through the wilderness from Haverhill to Penacook. In the fall of 1727, the first family, that of Captain Ebenezer Eastman, moved into the place. His team was driven by Jacob Shute, who was by birth a Frenchman, and he is said to have been the first person who drove a team through the wilderness. Soon after, says tradition, one Ayer, a lad of eighteen drove a team consisting of ten yoke of oxen to Penacook, swam the river, and ploughed a portion of the intervale. He is supposed to have been the first person who ploughed land in that place. After he had completed his work, he started on his return at sunrise, drowned a yoke of oxen while recrossing the river, and arrived at Haverhill about midnight. The crank of the first saw-mill was manufactured in Haverhill, and carried to Penacook on a horse."[1]

But we found that the frontiers were not this way any longer. This generation has come into the world fatally late for some enterprises. Go where we will on the *surface* of things, men have been there before us. We cannot now have the pleasure of erecting the *last* house; that was long ago set up in the suburbs of Astoria City, and our boundaries have literally been run to the South Sea, according to the old patents. But the lives of men, though more extended laterally in their range, are still as shallow as ever. Undoubtedly, as a Western orator said, "Men

[1] *The History of Haverhill, Massachusetts,* by B. L. Mirick, Haverhill, 1832, pages 145–146.

generally live over about the same surface; some live long and narrow, and others live broad and short;" but it is all superficial living.

A worm is as good a traveler as a grasshopper or a cricket, and a much wiser settler. With all their activity these do not hop away from drought nor forward to summer. We do not avoid evil by fleeing before it, but by rising above or diving below its plane; as the worm escapes drought and frost by boring a few inches deeper. The frontiers are not east or west, north or south, but wherever a man *fronts* a fact, though that fact be his neighbor, there is an unsettled wilderness between him and Canada, between him and the setting sun, or, farther still, between him and *it*. Let him build himself a log-house with the bark on where he is, *fronting* IT, and wage there an Old French war for seven or seventy years, with Indians and Rangers, or whatever else may come between him and the reality, and save his scalp if he can.

We now no longer sailed or floated on the river, but trod the unyielding land like pilgrims. Sadi tells who may travel; among others, "A common mechanic, who can earn a subsistence by the industry of his hand, and shall not have to stake his reputation for every morsel of bread, as philosophers have said."

He may travel who can subsist on the wild fruits and game of the most cultivated country. A man may travel fast enough and earn his living on the road. I have at times been applied to, to do work when on a journey; to do tinkering and repair clocks, when I had a knapsack on my back. A man once applied to me to go into a factory, stating conditions and wages, observing that I succeeded in shutting the window of a railroad car in which we were traveling, when the other passengers had failed. "Hast thou not heard of a Sufi, who was hammering some nails into the sole of his sandal; an officer of cavalry took him by the sleeve, saying, Come along and shoe my horse."

Farmers have asked me to assist them in haying when I was passing their fields. A man once applied to me to mend his umbrella, taking me for an umbrella-mender, because, being on a journey, I carried an umbrella in my hand while the sun shone. Another wished to buy a tin cup of me, observing that I had one strapped to my belt, and a sauce-pan on my back. The cheapest way to travel, and the way to travel the farthest in the shortest distance, is to go afoot, carrying a dipper, a spoon, and a fish-line, some Indian meal, some salt, and some sugar. When you come to a brook or pond, you can catch fish and cook them; or you can boil a hasty-pudding; or you can buy a loaf of bread at a farmer's house for fourpence, moisten it in the next brook that crosses the road, and dip into it your sugar, — this alone will last you a whole day; — or, if you are accustomed to heartier living, you can buy a quart of milk for two cents, crumb your bread or cold pudding into it, and eat it with your own spoon out of your own dish. Any one of these things I mean, not all together.

I have traveled thus some hundreds of miles without taking any meal in a house, sleeping on the ground when convenient, and found it cheaper, and in many respects more profitable, than staying at home. So that some have inquired why it would not be best to travel always. But I never thought of traveling simply as a means of getting a livelihood. A simple woman down in Tyngsborough, at whose house I once stopped to get a draught of water, when I said, recognizing the bucket, that I had stopped there nine years before for the same purpose, asked if I was not a traveler, supposing that I had been traveling ever since, and had now come round again; that traveling was one of the professions, more or less productive, which her husband did not follow.

But continued traveling is far from productive. It begins with wearing away the soles of the shoes, and making the feet sore, and erelong it will wear a man clean up, after making his heart sore into the bargain. I have observed that the after-life of those who have traveled much is very pathetic. True and sincere traveling is no pastime, but it is as serious as the grave, or any part of the human journey, and it requires a long probation to be broken into it. I do not speak of those that travel sitting, the sedentary travelers whose legs hang dangling the while, mere idle symbols of the fact, any more than when we speak of sitting hens we mean those that sit standing, but I mean those to whom traveling is life for the legs, and death too, at last. The traveler must be born again on the road, and earn a passport from the elements, the principal powers that be for him. He shall experience at last that old threat of his mother fulfilled, that he shall be skinned alive. His sores shall gradually deepen themselves that they may heal inwardly, while he gives no rest to the sole of his foot, and at night weariness must be his pillow, that so he may acquire experience against his rainy days. So was it with us.

Sometimes we lodged at an inn in the woods, where trout fishers from distant cities had arrived before us, and where, to our astonishment, the settlers dropped in at nightfall to have a chat and hear the news, though there was but one road, and no other house was visible, — as if they had come out of the earth.[1] There we sometimes read old newspapers, who never before read new ones, and in the rustle of their leaves heard the dashing of the surf along the Atlantic shore, instead of the sough of the wind among the pines. But then walking had given us an appetite even for the least palatable and nutritious food.

Some hard and dry book in a dead language, which you have found it impossible to read at home, but for

---

[1] Thoreau's Journal reveals that they had walked from their camp below Hooksett to Concord, a distance of ten miles. Here they spent the night. From thence they had come the next day — Friday — by stage forty miles to Plymouth; and then again taking to shanks' mare, they proceeded to Tilton's Inn in Thornton.

which you have still a lingering regard, is the best to carry with you on a journey. At a country inn, in the barren society of ostlers and travelers, I could undertake the writers of the silver or the brazen age with confidence. Almost the last regular service which I performed in the cause of literature was to read the works of Aulus Persius Flaccus.

Suns rose and set and found us still on the dank forest path which meanders up the Pemigewasset, now more like an otter's or a marten's trail, or where a beaver had dragged his trap, than where the wheels of travel raise a dust; where towns begin to serve as gores, only to hold the earth together. The wild pigeon sat secure above our heads, high on the dead limbs of naval pines, reduced to a robin's size. The very yards of our hostelries inclined upon the skirts of mountains, and, as we passed, we looked up at a steep angle at the stems of maples waving in the clouds.

Far up in the country, — for we would be faithful to our experience, — in Thornton, perhaps, we met a soldier lad in the woods, going to muster in full regimentals, and holding the middle of the road; deep in the forest, with shouldered musket and military step, and thoughts of war and glory all to himself. It was a sore trial to the youth, tougher than many a battle, to get by us creditably and with soldier-like bearing. Poor man! He actually shivered like a reed in his thin military pants, and by the time we had got up with him, all the sternness that becomes the soldier had forsaken his face, and he skulked past as if he were driving his father's sheep under a sword-proof helmet. It was too much for him to carry any extra armor then, who could not easily dispose of his natural arms. And for his legs, they were like heavy artillery in boggy places; better to cut the traces and forsake them. His greaves chafed and wrestled one with another for want of other foes. But he did get by and get off with all his munitions, and lived to fight another day; and I do not record this as casting any suspicion on his honor and real bravery in the field.

Wandering on through notches which the streams had made, by the side and over the brows of hoar hills and mountains, across the stumpy, rocky, forested, and bepastured country, we at length crossed on prostrate trees over the Amonoosuck, and breathed the free air of Unap-

propriated Land. Thus, in fair days as well as foul, we had traced up the river to which our native stream is a tributary, until from Merrimack it became the Pemigewasset that leaped by our side, and when we had passed its fountain-head, the Wild Amonoosuck, whose puny channel was crossed at a stride, guiding us toward its distant source among the mountains, at length, without its guidance, we were enabled to reach the summit of Agiocochook.[1]

When we returned to Hooksett, a week afterward, the melon man, in whose corn-barn we had hung our tent and buffaloes and other things to dry, was already picking his hops, with many women and children to help him. We

[1] Mount Washington. From the Journal it further appears after leaving Thornton they had passed through Peeling (now Woodstock) to Lincoln, where they visited the Stone Flume and Basin. From there they went on to Franconia — exploring the Notch and having their view of the Old Man of the Mountain. Here apparently they spent Saturday night, proceeding on Sunday to Crawford's. On Tuesday they "ascended the mountain" that is Agiocochook — Mount Washington. Their trip took them as far as Conway, whence they returned riding by way of Concord and arriving at Hookset on Thursday, September 12, 1839. In an entry in the following year, the whole excursion is referred to as "our White Mountain expedition." To those who know their White Mountains it will be obvious that this excursion of the Thoreau brothers lay almost exactly in the line of the now popular automobile route which follows up the courses of the Merrimack and the Pemigewasset — U.S. 3 — converging with that which, tracing through the mountains, follows down alongside the Saco River — U.S. 302 — to join near Conway with U.S. 16, from whence Route 25, passing between Squam Lake and Lake Winnepesaukee, carries one back into U.S. 3 and on down to Concord and Hookset. In 1839 Henry and his brother had been gone a week. Today their "White Mountain expedition" is a fair day's motor trip.

bought one watermelon, the largest in his patch, to carry with us for ballast. It was Nathan's, which he might sell if he wished, having been conveyed to him in the green state, and owned daily by his eyes. After due consultation with "Father," the bargain was concluded, — we to buy it at a venture on the vine, green or ripe, our risk, and pay "what the gentlemen pleased." It proved to be ripe; for we had had honest experience in selecting this fruit.

Finding our boat safe in its harbor, under Uncannunuc Mountain, with a fair wind and the current in our favor, we commenced our return voyage at noon, sitting at our ease and conversing, or in silence watching for the last trace of each reach in the river as a bend concealed it from our view. As the season was further advanced, the wind now blew steadily from the north, and with our sail set we could occasionally lie on our oars without loss of time.

The lumbermen throwing down wood from the top of the high bank, thirty or forty feet above the water, that it might be sent downstream, paused in their work to watch our retreating sail. By this time, indeed, we were well known to the boatmen, and were hailed as the Revenue Cutter of the stream. As we sailed rapidly down the river, shut in between two mounds of earth, the sounds of this timber rolled down the bank enhanced the silence and vastness of the noon, and we fancied that only the primeval echoes were awakened. The vision of a distant scow just heaving in sight round a headland also increased by contrast the solitude.

Through the din and desultoriness of noon, even in the most Oriental city, is seen the fresh and primitive and savage nature, in which Scythians and Ethiopians and Indians dwell. What is echo, what are light and shade, day and night, ocean and stars, earthquake and eclipse, there? The works of man are everywhere swallowed up in the immensity of nature. The Ægean Sea is but Lake Huron still to the Indian. Also there is all the refinement of civilized life in the woods under a sylvan garb. The wildest scenes have an air of domesticity and homeliness even to the citizen, and when the flicker's cackle is heard in the clearing, he is reminded that civilization has wrought but little change there. Science is welcome to the deepest recesses of the forest, for there too nature obeys the same old civil laws.

The little red bug on the stump of a pine, — for it the wind shifts and the sun breaks through the clouds. In the wildest nature, there is not only the material of the most cultivated life, and a sort of anticipation of the last result, but a greater refinement already than is ever attained by man. There is papyrus by the river-side, and rushes for light, and the goose only flies overhead, ages before the studious are born or letters invented, and that literature which the former suggest, and even from the first have rudely served, it may be man does not yet use them to express. Nature is prepared to welcome into her scenery the finest work of human art, for she is herself an art so cunning that the artist never appears in his work.

Art is not tame, and Nature is not wild, in the ordinary sense. A perfect work of man's art would also be wild or natural in a good sense. Man tames Nature only that he may at last make her more free even than he found her, though he may never yet have succeeded.

With this propitious breeze, and the help of our oars, we soon reached the Falls of Amoskeag, and the mouth of the Piscataquoag, and recognized, as we swept rapidly by, many a fair bank and islet on which our eyes had rested in the upward passage. Our boat was like that which Chaucer describes in his Dream, in which the knight took his departure from the island.

So we sailed this afternoon, thinking of the saying of Pythagoras, though we had no peculiar right to remember it, "It is beautiful when prosperity is present with intellect, and when sailing as it were with a prosperous wind, actions are performed looking to virtue; just as a pilot looks to the motions of the stars."

All the world reposes in beauty to him who preserves equipoise in his life, and moves serenely on his path without secret violence; as he who sails down a stream, he has only to steer, keeping his bark in the middle, and carry it round the falls. The ripples curled away in our wake, like ringlets from the head of a child, while we steadily held on our course.

The forms of beauty fall naturally around the path of

him who is in the performance of his proper work; as the curled shavings drop from the plane, and borings cluster round the auger. Undulation is the gentlest and most ideal of motions, produced by one fluid falling on another. Rippling is a more graceful flight. From a hill-top you may detect in it the wings of birds endlessly repeated. The two waving lines which represent the flight of birds appear to have been copied from the ripple.

The trees made an admirable fence to the landscape, skirting the horizon on every side. The single trees and the groves left standing on the intervale appeared naturally disposed, though the farmer had consulted only his convenience, for he too falls into the scheme of Nature. Art can never match the luxury and superfluity of Nature. In the former all is seen; it cannot afford concealed wealth, and is niggardly in comparison; but Nature, even when she is scant and thin outwardly, satisfies us still by the assurance of a certain generosity at the roots.

In swamps, where there is only here and there an evergreen tree amid the quaking moss and cranberry beds, the bareness does not suggest poverty. The single-spruce, which I had hardly noticed in gardens, attracts me in such places, and now first I understand why men try to make them grow about their houses. But though there may be very perfect specimens in front-yard plots, their beauty is for the most part ineffectual there, for there is no such assurance of kindred wealth beneath and around them, to make them show to advantage. As we have said, Nature is a greater and more perfect art, the art of God; though, referred to herself, she is genius; and there is a similarity between her operations and man's art even in the details and trifles.

When the overhanging pine drops into the water, by the sun and water, and the wind rubbing it against the shore, its boughs are worn into fantastic shapes, and white and smooth, as if turned in a lathe. Man's art has wisely imitated those forms into which all matter is most inclined to run, as foliage and fruit. A hammock swung in a grove assumes the exact form of a canoe, broader or narrower, and higher or lower at the ends, as more or fewer persons are in it, and it rolls in the air with the motion of the body, like a canoe in the water. Our art leaves its shavings and its dust about; her art exhibits itself even in the shavings and the dust which we make. She has perfected herself by an eternity of practice.

The world is well kept; no rubbish accumulates; the morning air is clear even at this day, and no dust has settled on the grass. Behold how the evening now steals over the fields, the shadows of the trees creeping farther and farther into the meadow, and erelong the stars will come to bathe in these retired waters. Her undertakings are secure and never fail. If I were awakened from a deep sleep, I should know which side of the meridian the sun might be by the aspect of nature, and by the chirp of the crickets, and yet no painter can paint this difference. The landscape contains a thousand dials which indicate the natural divisions of time, the shadows of a thousand styles point to the hour.

It is almost the only game which the trees play at, this tit-for-tat, now this side in the sun, now that, the drama of the day. In deep ravines under the eastern sides of cliffs, Night forwardly plants her foot even at noonday, and as Day retreats she steps into his trenches, skulking from tree to tree, from fence to fence, until at last she sits in his citadel and draws out her forces into the plain. It may be that the forenoon is brighter than the afternoon, not only because of the greater transparency of its atmosphere, but because we naturally look most into the west, as forward into the day, and so in the forenoon see the sunny side of things, but in the afternoon the shadow of every tree.

The afternoon is now far advanced, and a fresh and leisurely wind is blowing over the river, making long reaches of bright ripples. The river has done its stint, and appears not to flow, but lie at its length reflecting the light, and the haze over the woods is like the inaudible panting, or rather the gentle perspiration of resting nature, rising from a myriad of pores into the attenuated atmosphere.

On the thirty-first day of March, one hundred and forty-two years before this, probably about this time in the afternoon, there were hurriedly paddling down this part of the river, between the pine woods which then fringed these banks, two white women and a boy, who had left an island at the mouth of the Contoocook before daybreak. They were slightly clad for the season, in the English fashion, and handled their paddles unskillfully, but with nervous energy and determination, and at the bottom of their canoe lay the still bleeding scalps of ten of the aborigines.

They were Hannah Dustan, and her nurse, Mary Neff, both of Haverhill, eighteen miles from the mouth of this river, and an English boy, named Samuel Lennardson, escaping from captivity among the Indians. On the 15th of March previous, Hannah Dustan had been compelled to rise from childbed, and half dressed, with one foot bare, accompanied by her nurse, commence an uncertain march in still inclement weather, through the snow and the wilderness. She had seen her seven elder children flee with their father, but knew not of their fate. She had seen her infant's brains dashed out against an apple-tree, and had left her own and her neighbors' dwellings in ashes. When she reached the wigwam of her captor, situated on an island in the Merrimack, more than twenty miles above where we now are, she had been told that she and her nurse were soon to be taken to a distant Indian settlement, and there made to run the gauntlet naked.

The family of this Indian consisted of two men, three women, and seven children, besides an English boy, whom she found a prisoner among them. Having determined to attempt her escape, she instructed the boy to inquire of one of the men, how he should dispatch an enemy in the quickest manner, and take his scalp. "Strike 'em there," said he, placing his finger on his temple, and he also showed him how to take off the scalp. On the morning of the 31st she arose before daybreak, and awoke her nurse and the boy, and taking the Indians' tomahawks, they killed them all in their sleep, excepting one favorite boy, and one squaw who fled wounded with him to the

woods. The English boy struck the Indian who had given him the information, on the temple, as he had been directed.

They then collected all the provision they could find,

and took their master's tomahawk and gun, and scuttling all the canoes but one, commenced their flight to Haverhill, distant about sixty miles by the river. But after having proceeded a short distance, fearing that her story would not be believed if she should escape to tell it, they returned to the silent wigwam, and taking off the scalps of the dead, put them into a bag as proofs of what they had done, and then, retracing their steps to the shore in the twilight, recommenced their voyage.

Early this morning this deed was performed, and now, perchance, these tired women and this boy, their clothes stained with blood, and their minds racked with alternate resolution and fear, are making a hasty meal of parched corn and moose-meat, while their canoe glides under these pine roots whose stumps are still standing on the bank. They are thinking of the dead whom they have left behind on that solitary isle far up the stream, and of the relentless living warriors who are in pursuit. Every withered leaf which the winter has left seems to know their story, and in its rustling to repeat it and betray them. An Indian lurks behind every rock and pine, and their nerves cannot bear the tapping of a woodpecker. Or they forget their own dangers and their deeds in conjecturing the fate of their kindred, and whether, if they escape the Indians, they shall find the former still alive.

They do not stop to cook their meals upon the bank, nor land, except to carry their canoe about the falls. The stolen birch forgets its master and does them good service, and the swollen current bears them swiftly along with little need of the paddle, except to steer and keep them warm by exercise. For ice is floating in the river; the spring is opening; the musk-rat and the beaver are driven out of their holes by the flood; deer gaze at them from the bank; a few faint-singing forest birds, perchance, fly across the river to the northernmost shore; the fish-hawk sails and screams overhead, and geese fly over with a startling clangor; but they do not observe these things, or they speedily forget them. They do not smile or chat all day.

Sometimes they pass an Indian grave surrounded by its paling on the bank, or the frame of a wigwam, with a few coals left behind, or the withered stalks still rustling in the Indian's solitary cornfield on the intervale. The birch stripped of its bark, or the charred stump where a tree has been burned down to be made into a canoe, these are the only traces of man, a fabulous wild man to us. On either side, the primeval forest stretches away uninterrupted to Canada, or the "South Sea;" to the white man a drear and howling wilderness, but to the Indian a home, adapted to his nature, and cheerful as the smile of the Great Spirit.

While we loiter here this autumn evening, looking for a spot retired enough, where we shall quietly rest to-night, they thus, in that chilly March evening, one hundred and forty-two years before us, with wind and current favoring, have already glided out of sight, not to camp, as we shall, at night, but while two sleep one will manage the canoe, and the swift stream bear them onward to the settlements, it may be, even to old John Lovewell's house on Salmon Brook to-night.

According to the historian, they escaped as by a miracle all roving bands of Indians, and reached their homes in safety, with their trophies, for which the General Court paid them fifty pounds.[1] The family of Hannah Dustan all assembled alive once more, except the infant whose brains were dashed out against the apple-tree, and there have been many who in later times have lived to say that they had eaten of the fruit of that apple-tree.

This seems a long while ago, and yet it happened since Milton wrote his Paradise Lost. But its antiquity is not the less great for that, for we do not regulate our historical time by the English standard, nor did the English by the Roman, nor the Roman by the Greek. "We must look a long way back," says Raleigh, "to find the Romans giving laws to nations, and their consuls bringing kings and princes bound in chains to Rome in triumph; to see men go to Greece for wisdom, or Ophir for gold; when now nothing remains but a poor paper remembrance of their former condition."

And yet, in one sense, not so far back as to find the Penacooks and Pawtuckets using bows and arrows and

---

[1] This extraordinary tale is indubitably true. Knowledge of it was widespread at the time. The account is probably taken from Mirick's *History of Haverhill* (supra page 79) pages 86–92. Hannah "Dustan" [Dustin] is perpetrated in bronze in a public square in Haverhill.

hatchets of stone, on the banks of the Merrimack. From this September afternoon, and from between these now cultivated shores, those times seemed more remote than the dark ages. On beholding an old picture of Concord, as it appeared but seventy-five years ago, with a fair open prospect and a light on trees and river, as if it were broad noon, I find that I had not thought the sun shone in those days, or that men lived in broad daylight then. Still less do we imagine the sun shining on hill and valley during Philip's war, on the war-path of Church or Philip, or later of Lovewell or Paugus, with serene summer weather, but they must have lived and fought in a dim twilight or night.

Thus we "sayled by thought and pleasaunce," as Chaucer says, and all things seemed with us to flow; the shore itself and the distant cliffs were dissolved by the undiluted air. The hardest material seemed to obey the same law with the most fluid, and so indeed in the long run it does. Trees were but rivers of sap and woody fibre, flowing from the atmosphere, and emptying into the earth by their trunks, as their roots flowed upward to the surface. And in the heavens there were rivers of stars, and milky ways, already beginning to gleam and ripple over our heads. There were rivers of rock on the surface of the earth, and rivers of ore in its bowels, and our thoughts flowed and circulated, and this portion of time was but the current hour. Let us wander where we will, the universe is built round about us, and we are central still. If we look into the heavens they are concave, and if we were to look into a gulf as bottomless, it would be concave also. The sky is curved downward to the earth in the horizon, because we stand on the plain. I draw down its skirts. The stars so low there seem loath to depart, but by a circuitous path to be remembering me, and returning on their steps.

We had already passed by broad daylight the scene of our encampment at Coos Falls, and at length we pitched our camp on the west bank, in the northern part of Merrimack, nearly opposite to the large island on which we had spent the noon in our way up the river.

There we went to bed that summer evening, on a sloping shelf in the bank, a couple of rods from our boat, which was drawn up on the sand, and just behind a thin fringe of oaks which bordered the river; without having disturbed any inhabitants but the spiders in the grass, which came out by the light of our lamp, and crawled over our buffaloes. When we looked out from under the tent, the trees were seen dimly through the mist, and a cool dew hung upon the grass, which seemed to rejoice in the night, and with the damp air we inhaled a solid fragrance. Having eaten our supper of hot cocoa and bread and watermelon, we soon grew weary of conversing, and writing in our journals, and, putting out the lantern which hung from the tentpole, fell asleep.

Unfortunately, many things have been omitted which

should have been recorded in our journal; for though we made it a rule to set down all our experiences therein, yet such a resolution is very hard to keep, for the important experience rarely allows us to remember such obligations, and so indifferent things get recorded, while that is frequently neglected. It is not easy to write in a journal what interests us at any time, because to write it is not what interests us.

Whenever we awoke in the night, still eking out our dreams with half-awakened thoughts, it was not till after an interval, when the wind breathed harder than usual, flapping the curtains of the tent, and causing its cords to vibrate, that we remembered that we lay on the bank of the Merrimack, and not in our chamber at home. With our heads so low in the grass, we heard the river whirling and sucking, and lapsing downward, kissing the shore as it went, sometimes rippling louder than usual, and again its mighty current making only a slight limpid, trickling sound, as if our water-pail had sprung a leak, and the water were flowing into the grass by our side. The wind, rustling the oaks and hazels, impressed us like a wakeful and inconsiderate person up at midnight, moving about, and putting things to rights, occasionally stirring up whole drawers full of leaves at a puff.

There seemed to be a great haste and preparation throughout Nature, as for a distinguished visitor; all her aisles had to be swept in the night by a thousand handmaidens, and a thousand pots to be boiled for the next day's feasting; — such a whispering bustle, as if ten thousand fairies made their fingers fly, silently sewing at the new carpet with which the earth was to be clothed, and the new drapery which was to adorn the trees. And then the wind would lull and die away, and we like it fell asleep again.

8. Friday

As we lay awake long before daybreak, listening to the rippling of the river and the rustling of the leaves, in suspense whether the wind blew up or down the stream, was favorable or unfavorable to our voyage, we already suspected that there was a change in the weather, from a freshness as of autumn in these sounds. The wind in the woods sounded like an incessant waterfall dashing and roaring amid rocks, and we even felt encouraged by the unusual activity of the elements. He who hears the rippling of rivers in these degenerate days will not utterly despair. That night was the turning-point in the season. We had gone to bed in summer, and we awoke in autumn; for summer passes into autumn in some unimaginable point of time, like the turning of a leaf.

We found our boat in the dawn just as we had left it, and as if waiting for us, there on the shore, in autumn, all cool and dripping with dew, and our tracks still fresh in the wet sand around it, the fairies all gone or concealed. Before five o'clock we pushed it into the fog, and, leaping in, at one shove were out of sight of the shores, and began to sweep downward with the rushing river, keeping a sharp lookout for rocks. We could see only the yellow gurgling water, and a solid bank of fog on every side, forming a small yard around us. We soon passed the mouth of the Souhegan, and the village of Merrimack, and as the mist gradually rolled away, and we were relieved from the trouble of watching for rocks, we saw by the flitting clouds, by the first russet tinge on the hills, by the rushing river, the cottages on shore, and the shore itself, so coolly fresh and shining with dew, and later in the day, by the hue of the grape-vine, the goldfinch on the willow, the flickers flying in flocks, and when we passed near enough to the shore, as we fancied, by the faces of men, that the Fall had commenced. The cottages looked more snug and comfortable, and their inhabitants were seen only for a moment, and then went quietly in and shut the door, retreating inward to the haunts of summer.

We heard the sigh of the first autumnal wind, and even

the water had acquired a grayer hue. The sumach, grape, and maple were already changed, and the milkweed had turned to a deep, rich yellow. In all woods the leaves were fast ripening for their fall; for their full veins and lively gloss mark the ripe leaf and not the sered one of the poets; and we knew that the maples, stripped of their leaves among the earliest, would soon stand like a wreath of smoke along the edge of the meadow. Already the cattle were heard to low wildly in the pastures and along the highways, restlessly running to and fro, as if in apprehension of the withering of the grass and of the approach of winter. Our thoughts, too, began to rustle.

As I pass along the streets of our village of Concord on the day of our annual Cattle-Show, when it usually happens that the leaves of the elms and buttonwoods begin first to strew the ground under the breath of the October wind, the lively spirits in their sap seem to mount as high as any plough-boy's let loose that day; and they lead my thoughts away to the rustling woods, where the trees are preparing for their winter campaign. This autumnal festival, when men are gathered in crowds in the streets as regularly and by as natural a law as the leaves cluster and rustle by the wayside, is naturally associated in my mind with the fall of the year.

The low of cattle in the streets sounds like a hoarse symphony or running bass to the rustling of the leaves. The wind goes hurrying down the country, gleaning every loose straw that is left in the fields, while every farmer lad too appears to scud before it, — having donned his best pea-jacket and pepper-and-salt waistcoat, his unbent trousers, outstanding rigging of duck or kerseymere or corduroy, and his furry hat withal, — to country fairs and cattle-shows, to that Rome among the villages where the treasures of the year are gathered. All the land over they go leaping the fences with their tough, idle palms, which have never learned to hang by their sides, amid the low of calves and the bleating of sheep, — Amos, Abner, Elnathan, Elbridge, — "From steep pine-bearing mountains to the plain."

I love these sons of earth, every mother's son of them, with their great hearty hearts rushing tumultuously in herds from spectacle to spectacle, as if fearful lest there should not be time between sun and sun to see them all, and the sun does not wait more than in haying-time.

Running hither and thither with appetite for the coarse pastimes of the day, now with boisterous speed at the heels of the inspired negro from whose larynx the melodies of all Congo and Guinea Coast have broke loose into our streets; now to see the procession of a hundred yoke of oxen, all as august and grave as Osiris, or the droves of neat cattle and milch cows as unspotted as Isis or Io. Such as had no love for Nature "at all, came lovers home from this great festival." They may bring their fattest cattle and richest fruits to the fair, but they are all eclipsed by the show of men.

These are stirring autumn days, when men sweep by in crowds, amid the rustle of leaves, like migrating finches; this is the true harvest of the year, when the air is but the breath of men, and the rustling of leaves is as the trampling of the crowd. We read nowadays of the ancient festivals, games, and processions of the Greeks and Etruscans with a little incredulity, or at least with little sympathy; but how natural and irrepressible in every people is some hearty and palpable greeting of Nature. The Corybantes, the Bacchantes, the rude primitive tragedians with their procession and goat-song, and the whole paraphernalia of the Panathenæa, which appear so antiquated and peculiar, have their parallel now. The husbandman is always a better Greek than the scholar is prepared to appreciate, and the old custom still survives, while antiquarians and scholars grow gray in commemorating it. The farmers crowd to the fair to-day in obedience to the same ancient law, which Solon or Lycurgus did not enact, as naturally as bees swarm and follow their queen.

It is worth the while to see the country's people, how they pour into the town, the sober farmer folk, now all agog, their very shirt and coat collars pointing forward, — collars so broad as if they had put their shirts on wrong end upward, for the fashions always tend to superfluity, — and with an unusual springiness in their gait, jabbering earnestly to one another. The more supple vagabond, too, is sure to appear on the least rumor of such a gathering, and the next day to disappear, and go into his hole like the seventeen-year locust, in an ever-shabby coat, though finer than the farmer's best, yet never dressed; come to see the sport, and have a hand in what is going, — to know "what's the row," if there is any; to be where some men are drunk, some horses race, some cockerels fight; anxious to be shaking props under a table, and above all to see the "striped pig." He especially is the creature of the occasion. He empties both his pockets and his character into the stream, and swims in such a day. He dearly loves the social slush. There is no reserve of soberness in him.

I love to see the herd of men feeding heartily on coarse and succulent pleasures, as cattle on the husks and stalks of vegetables. Though there are many crooked and crabbed specimens of humanity among them, run all to thorn and rind, and crowded out of shape by adverse circumstances, like the third chestnut in the burr, so that you wonder to see some heads wear a whole hat, yet fear not that the race will fail or waver in them; like the crabs which grow in hedges, they furnish the stocks of sweet and thrifty fruits still. Thus is nature recruited from age to age, while the fair and palatable varieties die out, and have their period. This is that mankind. How cheap must be the material of which so many men are made.

The wind blew steadily down the stream, so that we kept our sails set, and lost not a moment of the forenoon by delays, but from early morning until noon were con-

tinually dropping downward. With our hands on the steering-paddle, which was thrust deep into the river, or bending to the oar, which indeed we rarely relinquished, we felt each palpitation in the veins of our steed, and each impulse of the wings which drew us above. The current of our thoughts made as sudden bends as the river, which was continually opening new prospects to the east or south, but we are aware that rivers flow most rapidly and shallowest at these points. The steadfast shores never once turned aside for us, but still trended as they were made; why then should we always turn aside for them?

While we sailed fleetly before the wind, with the river gurgling under our stern, the thoughts of autumn coursed as steadily through our minds, and we observed less what was passing on the shore, than the dateless associations and impressions which the season awakened, anticipating in some measure the progress of the year.

Sitting with our faces now upstream, we studied the landscape by degrees, as one unrolls a map — rock, tree, house, hill, and meadow, assuming new and varying positions as wind and water shifted the scene, and there was variety enough for our entertainment in the metamorphoses of the simplest objects. Viewed from this side the scenery appeared new to us.

The most familiar sheet of water, viewed from a new hill-top, yields a novel and unexpected pleasure. When we have traveled a few miles, we do not recognize the profiles even of the hills which overlook our native village, and perhaps no man is quite familiar with the horizon as seen from the hill nearest to his house, and can recall its outline distinctly when in the valley. We do not commonly know, beyond a short distance, which way the hills range which take in our houses and farms in their sweep. As if our birth had at first sundered things, and we had been thrust up through into nature like a wedge, and not till the wound heals and the scar disappears do we begin to discover where we are, and that nature is one and continuous everywhere. It is an important epoch when a man who has always lived on the east side of a mountain, and seen it in the west, travels round and sees it in the east.

Yet the universe is a sphere whose centre is wherever there is intelligence. The sun is not so central as a man. Upon an isolated hill-top, in an open country, we seem to ourselves to be standing on the boss of an immense shield, the immediate landscape being apparently depressed below the more remote, and rising gradually to the horizon, which is the rim of the shield, — villas, steeples, forests, mountains, one above another, till they are swallowed up in the heavens. The most distant mountains in the horizon appear to rise directly from the shore of that lake in the woods by which we chance to be standing, while from the mountain-top, not only this, but a thousand nearer and larger lakes, are equally unobserved.

Seen through this clear atmosphere, the works of the farmer, his ploughing and reaping, had a beauty to our eyes which he never saw. How fortunate were we who did not own an acre of these shores, who had not renounced our title to the whole. One who knew how to appropriate the true value of this world would be the poorest man in it. The poor rich man! all he has is what he has bought. What I see is mine. I am a large owner in the Merrimack intervales. He is the rich man, and enjoys the fruits of riches, who summer and winter forever can find delight in his own thoughts. Buy a farm! What have I to pay for a farm which a farmer will take?

When I visit again some haunt of my youth, I am glad to find that nature wears so well. The landscape is indeed something real, and solid, and sincere, and I have not put my foot through it yet. There is a pleasant tract on the bank of the Concord, called Conantum, which I have in my mind; — the old deserted farm-house, the desolate pasture with its bleak cliff, the open wood, the river-reach, the green meadow in the midst, and the moss-grown wild-apple orchard, — places where one may have many thoughts and not decide anything. It is a scene which I cannot only remember, as I might a vision, but when I will can bodily revisit, and find it even so, unaccountable, yet unpretending in its pleasant dreariness. When my thoughts are sensible of change, I love to see and sit on rocks which I *have* known, and pry into their moss, and see unchangeableness so established. I not yet gray on rocks forever gray, I no longer green under the evergreens. There is something even in the lapse of time by which time recovers itself.

As we have said, it proved a cool as well as breezy day, and by the time we reached Penichook Brook we were obliged to sit muffled in our cloaks, while the wind and current carried us along. We bounded swiftly over the rippling surface, far by many cultivated lands and the ends of fences which divided innumerable farms, with hardly a thought for the various lives which they separated; now by long rows of alders or groves of pines or oaks, and now by some homestead where the women and children stood outside to gaze at us, till we had swept out of their sight, and beyond the limit of their longest Saturday ramble. We glided past the mouth of the Nashua, and not long after, of Salmon Brook, without more pause than the wind.

The shadows chased one another swiftly over wood and meadow, and their alternation harmonized with our mood. We could distinguish the clouds which cast each one, though never so high in the heavens. When a shadow flits across the landscape of the soul, where is the substance? Probably, if we were wise enough, we should see to what virtue we are indebted for any happier moment we enjoy. No doubt we have earned it at some time; for the gifts of Heaven are never quite gratuitous. The constant abrasion and decay of our lives makes the soil of our future growth. The wood which we now mature, when it becomes virgin mould, determines the character of our second growth, whether that be oaks or pines.

Every man casts a shadow; not his body only, but his imperfectly mingled spirit. This is his grief. Let him turn which way he will, it falls opposite to the sun; short at noon, long at eve. Did you never see it? But, referred to the sun, it is widest at its base, which is no greater than his own opacity. The divine light is diffused almost entirely around us, and by means of the refraction of light, or else by a certain self-luminousness, or, as some will have it, transparency, if we preserve ourselves untarnished, we are able to enlighten our shaded side. At any rate, our darkest grief has that bronze color of the moon eclipsed. There is no ill which may not be dissipated, like the dark, if you let in a stronger light upon it. Shadows, referred to the source of light, are pyramids whose bases are never greater than those of the substances which cast them, but light is a spherical congeries of pyramids, whose very apexes are the sun itself, and hence the system shines with uninterrupted light. But if the light we use is but a paltry and narrow taper, most objects will cast a shadow wider than themselves.

The places where we had stopped or spent the night in our way up the river had already acquired a slight historical interest for us; for many upward days' voyaging were unraveled in this rapid downward passage. When one landed to stretch his limbs by walking, he soon found himself falling behind his companion, and was obliged to take advantage of the curves, and ford the brooks and ravines in haste, to recover his ground. Already the banks and the distant meadows wore a sober and deepened tinge, for the September air had shorn them of their summer's pride. The air was really the "fine element" which the poets describe. It had a finer and sharper grain, seen against the russet pastures and meadows, than before, as if cleansed of the summer's impurities.

Having passed the New Hampshire line and reached the Horseshoe Intervale in Tyngsborough, where there is a high and regular second bank, we climbed up this in haste to get a nearer sight of the autumnal flowers, asters, goldenrod, and yarrow, and blue-curls (*Trichostema dichotomum*), humble roadside blossoms, and, lingering still, the harebell and the *Rhexia Virginica.* The last growing in patches of lively pink flowers on the edge of the meadows, had almost too gay an appearance for the rest of the landscape, like a pink ribbon on the bonnet of a Puritan woman. Asters and goldenrods were the livery which nature wore at present. The latter alone expressed all the ripeness of the season, and shed their mellow lustre over the fields, as if the now declining summer's sun had bequeathed its hues to them. It is the floral solstice a little after midsummer, when the particles of golden light, the sun-dust, have, as it were, fallen like seeds on the earth, and produced these blossoms. On every hillside, and in every valley, stood countless asters, coreopses, tansies,

golden-rods, and the whole race of yellow flowers, like Brahminical devotees, turning steadily with their luminary from morning till night.

There is a peculiar interest belonging to the still later

flowers, which abide with us the approach of winter. There is something witch-like in the appearance of the witch hazel, which blossoms late in October and in November, with its irregular and angular spray and petals like furies' hair, or small ribbon streamers. Its blossoming, too, at this irregular period, when other shrubs have lost their leaves, as well as blossoms, looks like witches' craft. Certainly it blooms in no garden of man's. There is a whole fairy-land on the hillside where it grows.

Some have thought that the gales do not at present waft to the voyager the natural and original fragrance of the land, such as the early navigators described, and that the loss of many odoriferous native plants, sweet-scented grasses and medicinal herbs, which formerly sweetened the atmosphere, and rendered it salubrious, — by the grazing of cattle and the rooting of swine, is the source of many diseases which now prevail; the earth, say they, having been long subjected to extremely artificial and luxurious modes of cultivation, to gratify the appetite, converted into a stye and hot-bed, where men for profit increase the ordinary decay of nature.

According to the record of an old inhabitant of Tyngsborough, now dead, whose farm we were now gliding past, one of the greatest freshets on this river took place in October, 1785, and its height was marked by a nail driven into an apple-tree behind his house. One of his descendants has shown this to me, and I judged it to be at least seventeen or eighteen feet above the level of the river at the time. According to Barber the river rose twenty-one feet above the common high-water mark at Bradford in the year 1818.

Before the Lowell and Nashua railroad was built, the engineer made inquiries of the inhabitants along the banks as to how high they had known the river to rise. When he came to this house he was conducted to the apple-tree, and as the nail was not then visible, the lady of the house placed her hand on the trunk where she said that she remembered the nail to have been from her childhood. In the mean while the old man put his arm inside the tree, which was hollow, and felt the point of the nail sticking through, and it was exactly opposite to her hand. The spot is now plainly marked by a notch in the bark. But as no one else remembered the river to have risen so high as this, the engineer disregarded this statement, and I learn that there has since been a freshet which rose within nine inches of the rails at Biscuit Brook, and such a freshet as that of 1785 would have covered the railroad two feet deep.

The revolutions of nature tell as fine tales, and make as interesting revelations, on this river's banks, as on the Euphrates or the Nile. This apple-tree, which stands within a few rods of the river, is called "Elisha's apple-tree," from a friendly Indian, who was anciently in the service of Jonathan Tyng, and, with one other man, was killed here by his own race in one of the Indian wars, — the particulars of which affair were told us on the spot.

He was buried close by, no one knew exactly where, but in the flood of 1785, so great a weight of water standing over the grave caused the earth to settle where it had once been disturbed, and when the flood went down, a sunken spot, exactly of the form and size of the grave, revealed its locality; but this was now lost again, and no future flood can detect it; yet, no doubt, nature will know how to point it out in due time, if it be necessary, by methods yet more searching and unexpected. Thus there is not only the crisis when the spirit ceases to inspire and expand the body, marked by a fresh mound in the churchyard, but there is also a crisis when the body ceases to take up room as such in nature, marked by a fainter depression in the earth.

We sat awhile to rest here upon the brink of the western bank, surrounded by the glossy leaves of the red variety of the mountain laurel, just above the head of Wicasuck Island, where we could observe some scows which were loading with clay from the opposite shore, and also overlook the grounds of the farmer, of whom I have spoken, who once hospitably entertained us for a night. He had on his pleasant farm, besides an abundance of the beach-plum, or *Prunus littoralis,* which grew wild, the Canada plum under cultivation, fine Porter apples, some peaches, and large patches of musk and water melons, which he cultivated for the Lowell market.

Elisha's apple-tree, too, bore a native fruit, which was prized by the family; he raised the blood peach, which, as he showed us with satisfaction, was more like the oak in the color of its bark and in the setting of its branches, and was less liable to break down under the weight of the fruit, or the snow, than other varieties. It was of slower growth, and its branches strong and tough. There, also, was his nursery of native apple-trees, thickly set upon the bank, which cost but little care, and which he sold to the neighboring farmers when they were five or six years old. To see a single peach upon its stem makes an impression of paradisaical fertility and luxury. This reminded us even of an old Roman farm, as described by Varro: — "Cæsar Vopiscus Ædilicius, when he pleaded before the Censors, said that the grounds of Rosea were the garden (*sumen*, the tid-bit) of Italy, in which a pole being left would not be visible the day after, on account of the growth of the herbage." This soil may not have been remarkably fertile, yet at this distance we thought that this anecdote might be told of the Tyngsborough farm.

When we passed Wicasuck Island, there was a pleasure boat containing a youth and a maiden on the island brook, which we were pleased to see, since it proved that there were some hereabouts to whom our excursion would not be wholly strange. Before this, a canal-boatman, of whom we made some inquiries respecting Wicasuck Island, and who told us that it was disputed property, suspected that we had a claim upon it, and though we assured him that all this was news to us, and explained, as well as we could, why we had come to see it, he believed not a word of it, and seriously offered us one hundred dollars for our title. The only other small boats which we met with were used to pick up drift-wood. Some of the poorer class along the stream collect, in this way, all the fuel which they require. While one of us landed not far from this island to forage for provisions among the farm-houses whose roofs we saw, — for our supply was now exhausted, — the other, sitting in the boat, which was moored to the shore, was left alone to his reflections.

If there is nothing new on the earth, still the traveler always has a resource in the skies. They are constantly turning a new page to view. The wind sets the types on this blue ground, and the inquiring may always read a new truth there. There are things there written with such fine and subtile tinctures, paler than the juice of limes, that to the diurnal eye they leave no trace, and only the chemistry of night reveals them. Every man's daylight firmament answers in his mind to the brightness of the vision in his starriest hour.

These continents and hemispheres are soon run over, but an always unexplored and infinite region makes off on every side from the mind, further than to sunset, and we can make no highway or beaten track into it, but the grass immediately springs up in the path, for we travel there chiefly with our wings.

Sometimes we see objects as through a thin haze, in their eternal relations, and they stand like Palenque and the Pyramids, and we wonder who set them up, and for what purpose. If we see the reality in things, of what moment is the superficial and apparent longer? What are the earth and all its interests beside the deep surmise which pierces and scatters them? While I sit here listening to the waves which ripple and break on this shore, I am absolved from all obligations to the past, and the council of nations may reconsider its votes. The grating of a pebble annuls them. Still occasionally in my dreams I remember that rippling water.

With a bending sail we glided rapidly by Tyngsborough and Chelmsford, each holding in one hand half of a tart country apple-pie which we had purchased to celebrate our return, and in the other a fragment of the newspaper in which it was wrapped, devouring these with divided relish, and learning the news which had transpired since we sailed. The river here opened into a broad and straight reach of great length, which we bounded merrily over before a smacking breeze, with a devil-may-care look in our faces, and our boat a white bone in its mouth, and a speed which greatly astonished some scow boatmen whom we met.

The wind in the horizon rolled like a flood over valley and plain, and every tree bent to the blast, and the mountains like school-boys turned their cheeks to it. They were great and current motions, the flowing sail, the running stream, the waving tree, the roving wind. The north wind stepped readily into the harness which we had provided, and pulled us along with good will. Sometimes we sailed as gently and steadily as the clouds overhead, watching the receding shores and the motions of our sail; the play of its pulse so like our own lives, so thin and yet so full of life, so noiseless when it labored hardest, so noisy and impatient when least effective; now bending to some generous impulse of the breeze, and then fluttering and flapping with a kind of human suspense. It was the scale on which the varying temperature of distant atmospheres was graduated, and it was some attraction for us that the breeze it played with had been out of doors so long.

Thus we sailed, not being able to fly, but as next best, making a long furrow in the fields of the Merrimack toward our home, with our wings spread, but never lifting our heel from the watery trench; gracefully ploughing homeward with our brisk and willing team, wind and stream, pulling together, the former yet a wild steer, yoked to his more sedate fellow. It was very near flying, as when the duck rushes through the water with an impulse of her wings, throwing the spray about her before she can rise. How we had stuck fast if drawn up but a few feet on the shore!

When we reached the great bend just above Middlesex, where the river runs east thirty-five miles to the sea, we at length lost the aid of this propitious wind, though we contrived to make one long and judicious tack carry us nearly to the locks of the canal. We were here locked through at noon by our old friend, the lover of the higher mathematics, who seemed glad to see us safe back again through so many locks; but we did not stop to consider any of his problems, though we could cheerfully have spent a whole autumn in this way another time, and never have asked what his religion was. It is so rare to meet with a man out-doors who cherishes a worthy thought in his mind, which is independent of the labor of his hands. Behind every man's busy-ness there should be a level of undisturbed serenity and industry, as within the reef encircling a coral isle there is always an expanse of still water, where the depositions are going on which will finally raise it above the surface.

We endeavored in vain to persuade the wind to blow through the long corridor of the canal, which is here cut straight through the woods, and were obliged to resort to our old expedient of drawing by a cord. When we reached the Concord, we were forced to row once more in good earnest, with neither wind nor current in our favor, but by this time the rawness of the day had disappeared, and we experienced the warmth of a summer afternoon. This change in the weather was favorable to our contemplative mood, and disposed us to dream yet deeper at our oars, while we floated in imagination farther down the stream of time, as we had floated down the stream of the Merrimack, to poets of a milder period than had engaged us in the morning. Chelmsford and Billerica appeared like old English towns, compared with Merrimack and Nashua, and many generations of civil poets might have lived and sung here.

Thus thoughtfully we were rowing homeward to find some autumnal work to do, and help on the revolution of the seasons. Perhaps Nature would condescend to make use of us even without our knowledge, as when we help to scatter her seeds in our walks, and carry burrs and cockles on our clothes from field to field.

As it grew later in the afternoon, and we rowed leisurely up the gentle stream, shut in between fragrant and blooming banks, where we had first pitched our tent, and drew nearer to the fields where our lives had passed, we seemed to detect the hues of our native sky in the southwest horizon. The sun was just setting behind the edge of a wooded hill, so rich a sunset as would never have ended but for some reason unknown to men, and to be marked with brighter colors than ordinary in the scroll of time. Though the shadows of the hills were beginning to steal over the stream, the whole river valley undulated with mild light, purer and more memorable than the noon. For so day bids farewell even to solitary vales uninhabited by man.

Two blue-herons (*Ardea herodias*), with their long and slender limbs relieved against the sky, were seen traveling high over our heads, — their lofty and silent flight, as they were wending their way at evening, surely not to alight in any marsh on the earth's surface, but, perchance, on the other side of our atmosphere, a symbol for the

ages to study, whether impressed upon the sky, or sculptured amid the hieroglyphics of Egypt. Bound to some northern meadow, they held on their stately, stationary flight, like the storks in the picture, and disappeared at length behind the clouds. Dense flocks of blackbirds were winging their way along the river's course, as if on a short evening pilgrimage to some shrine of theirs, or to celebrate so fair a sunset.

The sun-setting presumed all men at leisure, and in a contemplative mood; but the farmer's boy only whistled the more thoughtfully as he drove his cows home from pasture, and the teamster refrained from cracking his whip, and guided his team with a subdued voice. The last vestiges of daylight at length disappeared, and as we rowed silently along with our banks toward home through the darkness, only a few stars being visible, we had little to say, but sat absorbed in thought, or in silence listened to the monotonous sound of our oars, a sort of rudimental music, suitable for the ear of Night and the acoustics of her dimly lighted halls. "*Pulsæ referunt ad sidera valles,*" — and the valleys echoed the sound to the stars.

As we looked up in silence to those distant lights, we were reminded that it was a rare imagination which first taught that the stars are worlds, and had conferred a great benefit on mankind. It is recorded in the Chronicle of Bernaldez that in Columbus's first voyage the natives "pointed toward the heavens, making signs that they believed that there was all power and holiness." We have reason to be grateful for celestial phenomena, for they chiefly answer to the ideal in man. The stars are distant and unobtrusive, but bright and enduring as our fairest and most memorable experiences. "Let the immortal depth of your soul lead you, but earnestly extend your eyes upwards."

As the truest society approaches always nearer to solitude, so the most excellent speech finally falls into Silence. Silence is audible to all men, at all times, and in all places. She is when we hear inwardly, sound when we hear outwardly. Creation has not displaced her, but is her visible framework and foil. All sounds are her servants, and purveyors, proclaiming not only that their mistress is, but is a rare mistress, and earnestly to be sought after. They are so far akin to Silence that they are but bubbles on her surface, which straightway burst, an evidence of the strength and prolificness of the under-current; a faint utterance of Silence, and then only agreeable to our auditory nerves when they contrast themselves with and relieve the former. In proportion as they do this, and are heighteners and intensifiers of the Silence, they are harmony and purest melody.

Silence is the universal refuge, the sequel to all dull discourses and all foolish acts, a balm to our every chagrin, as welcome after satiety as after disappointment; that background which the painter may not daub, be he master or bungler, and which, however awkward a figure we may have made in the foreground, remains ever our inviolable asylum, where no indignity can assail, no personality disturb us.

The orator puts off his individuality, and is then most eloquent when most silent. He listens while he speaks, and is a hearer along with his audience. Who has not hearkened to her infinite din? She is Truth's speaking-trumpet, the sole oracle, the true Delphi and Dodona, which kings and courtiers would do well to consult, nor will they be balked by an ambiguous answer. For through her all revelations have been made, and just in proportion as men have consulted her oracle within, they have obtained a clear insight, and their age has been marked as an enlightened one. But as often as they have gone gadding abroad to a strange Delphi and her mad priestess, their age has been dark and leaden. Such were garrulous and noisy eras, which no longer yield any sound, but the

Grecian or silent and melodious era is ever sounding and resounding in the ears of men.

A good book is the plectrum with which our else silent lyres are struck. We not unfrequently refer the interest which belongs to our own unwritten sequel to the written and comparatively lifeless body of the work. Of all books this sequel is the most indispensable part. It should be the author's aim to say once and emphatically, "He said," ἔφη. This is the most the bookmaker can attain to. If he make his volume a mole whereon the waves of Silence may break, it is well.

It were vain for me to endeavor to interpret the Silence. She cannot be done into English. For six thousand years men have translated her with what fidelity belonged to each, and still she is little better than a sealed book. A man may run on confidently for a time, thinking he has her under his thumb, and shall one day exhaust her, but he too must at last be silent, and men remark only how brave a beginning he made; for when he at length dives into her, so vast is the disproportion of the told to the untold that the former will seem but the bubble on the surface where he disappeared. Nevertheless, we will go on, like those Chinese cliff swallows, feathering our nests with the froth which may one day be bread of life to such as dwell by the seashore.

We had made about fifty miles this day with sail and oar, and now, far in the evening, our boat was grating

HENRY

against the bulrushes of its native port, and its keel recognized the Concord mud, where some semblance of its outline was still preserved in the flattened flags which had scarce yet erected themselves since our departure; and we leaped gladly on shore, drawing it up, and fastening it to the wild apple-tree, whose stem still bore the mark which its chain had worn in the chafing of the spring freshets.